Sunday Savers:
Sharing Fun! – 2017 Sharing Time Activities

Theme: Choose the Right

- 20 Learning Activities to Match Monthly Themes

(Theme 2—January sample is shown)

Princess and Prince
Choose the Right Consequence

Primary and Music Leaders:

DOWNLOAD from gospelgrabbag.com the following: (1) Monthly sharing time theme **Scripture Posters** and memorization cards, (2) **Song Visuals** to teach practice songs, (3) **Singing Activities** to motivate children to sing, (4) **Articles of Faith 1–13** posters and c[...] activities, invitations, and goal planners for every goal.

About the AUTHOR, ILLUSTRATOR:

Mary H. Ross, author, and Jennette Guymon-King, illustrator, have sold over one million LDS products published by Covenant Communications.

Mary H. Ross, Author

Jennette Guymon-King, Illustrator

You can reach them at gospelgrabbag.com.

Here you can view more of the *Sunday Savers* series books and CD-ROMs and download more activities. You will find 2017 "Choose the Right" theme scripture memorization posters, practice song visuals, and more. Don't miss the Faith in God Activity Days activities for every goal, including a matching invitation.

Don't miss the latest quiz decks:
1. *Book of Mormon Quiz-Bee* (shown left),
2. *Articles of Faith Quiz-Bee* (shown right).

These make great gifts for children who are being baptized or are graduating from Primary.

Copyright © 2016 by Mary H. Ross and Jennette Guymon-King—All Rights Reserved.
PUBLISHER: Covenant Communications, Inc., American Fork, Utah—First printing: November 2016

Sunday Savers™ *Sharing Fun: Choose the Right*
ISBN: 978-1-52440-167-2

INTRODUCTION

SHARING FUN—Sharing Time Activities
2017 Theme: Choose the Right

This volume of teaching ideas is designed for the 2017 Primary Sharing Time theme. Plus, it can be used year after year for family home evening lessons and Sharing Time themes that help children come to learn and say, **"Choose the Right."**

You will find 20 learning activities (one or two for every month of the year). Each is designed to present on a poster or board with visuals large enough for children to see and visualize the lessons taught. Each coordinates with the **"Choose the Right"** theme for that week/month. Example shown is the Friend Not Foe activity for July Sharing Time.

TO USE THE Sharing Fun BOOK: Copy the visuals, color, cut out, and follow instructions.

TO USE THE Sharing Fun CD-ROM: Print images found in this book from the CD-ROM (sold separately—shown left). They can be printed in color or black-and-white. Samples are shown on the back cover of this book.

FOR SINGING LEADERS: Song visuals to help you teach the 2017 practice songs are available to **download/print from gospelgrabbag.com** (sample shown right for the February theme: When We Choose the Right, We Are Blessed).

If ye do keep his commandments he doth bless you and prosper you.

Mosiah 2:22

CHOOSE THE RIGHT

SCRIPTURE MEMORIZATION: Monthly theme scriptures for the 2017 year are available to **download/print from gospelgrabbag.com.** They are in large posters or small cards to give children (sample shown left to match with February's sharing time theme).

LET CHILDREN TEACH: Older children can present the ideas for Sharing Time. **BEST OF ALL:** You can enjoy these activities for monthly family home evenings.

Don't miss the **Articles of Faith 1–13** scripture posters and cards to print from gospelgrabbag.com.

January—Theme 1: Agency Is the Gift to Choose for Ourselves

Practice Time:
Scripture Memorization—
2 Nephi 2:27 (shown left). Poster/cards (shown) are only available to <u>download from gospelgrabbag.com</u>.

Practice Song — Sing "As a Child of God" (*Friend*, Jan. 2012) using the song visuals (shown right). These are only available to <u>download from gospelgrabbag.com</u>.

AS A CHILD OF GOD

SHARING TIME, Weeks 1 and 2:
Agency Is the Gift to Choose for Ourselves

Activity 1: Choose the Right Consequences
(Build a True Prince & Princess Puzzle)

OBJECTIVE: Help children know that even though Heavenly Father has given us agency to choose for ourselves, He wants us to make right choices each day. This way we can be a true prince or princess and be crowned with glory. Right choices will help us be happy and free. Bad choices can bring misery and captivity.

TO MAKE VISUALS:
Copy, color, and cut out the images that follow. Laminate.

ACTIVITY:
1. Ahead of time, hide the cards by taping them under chairs or on a wall across the room.
2. Have children help you put the puzzle together as you talk about the prince's and princess's feet, legs, hands, arms, hearts, shoulders, and heads. Talk about how they can use these to create royal actions, then be crowned with glory if they are valiant. Tell children they are of royal birth, children of a living God who loves them. Heavenly Father wants us to make right choices so we can be part of His kingdom. We can find happiness only when we choose the right and keep all of Heavenly Father's commandments.

3. Have children find cards under chairs, then have all the feet cards start first, placing the feet position cards next to the feet position on the puzzle. Talk about the valiant choice and the good consequence for that action.

4. Repeat with each body part: legs, hands, arms, hearts, shoulders, and heads until you reach the crown, telling children that HEAVENLY FATHER WISHES TO CROWN US WITH GLORY FOR OUR ACTIONS.

Note: This can be done in two weeks by using half the cards, choosing some of each to discuss. Talk about the card action and the good consequence. Then tell the opposite bad action and the consequence.

Princess and Prince

Choose the Right Consequence

I will stand as a witness and share my testimony of Jesus.

I will walk quietly in church to show my reverence.

I will walk and not be weary as I keep the Word of Wisdom.

I will run home quickly when Mother or Father calls me.

I will strive to develop and share my talents.

I will walk away if I am tempted to do wrong.

I will shake hands and happily make new friends.

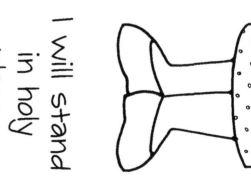

I will stand in holy places.

I will work hard to serve and help others.

I will live so the Holy Ghost can speak to my heart.

I will hug my family members to show my love.

I will be kindhearted to others.

I will fold my arms to pray and show my reverence to Heavenly Father.

I will pray to Heavenly Father with a sincere heart.

I will stretch out my arms to help the poor and needy.

I will stand tall and do what Jesus would do.

I will bear another's burdens and strive to comfort them.

I will stand tall and strive to be a good example.

I will read the scriptures.

I will watch movies that would be pleasing to Heavenly Father.

I will hear the teachings of the prophet and Apostles.

I will listen to the promptings of the Holy Ghost.

I will speak the truth at all times.

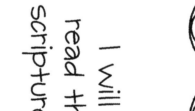

I will strive to always speak kindly to others.

I will speak of Heavenly Father and Jesus Christ reverently.

I will think of Heavenly Father's many blessings and be grateful.

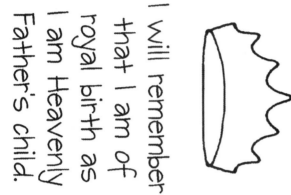

I will smile even when life gets difficult.

I will remember that I am of royal birth as I am Heavenly Father's child.

I will think good thoughts of others and myself.

I will be valiant in keeping the commandments so I can live in Heavenly Father's kingdom.

I will work to learn and excel in school.

I will be crowned with glory as I strive to follow Heavenly Father's plan for me.

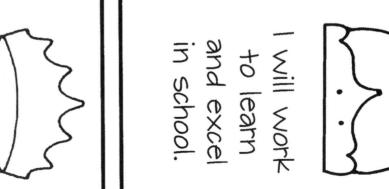

February—Theme 2: When We Choose The Right, We Are Blessed

If ye do keep his commandments he doth bless you and prosper you.

Mosiah 2:22

Practice Time:
Scripture Memorization —
Mosiah 2:22 (shown left). Poster/cards (shown) are only available to <u>download from gospelgrabbag.com</u>.

Practice Song — Sing "Choose the Right" (*Hymns*, no. 239) using the song visuals (shown right). These are only available to <u>download from gospelgrabbag.com</u>.

CHOOSE THE RIGHT

SHARING TIME, Week 1:
Noah Was Blessed for Choosing the Right

Activity: Choosing to Obey
(Noah, Ark, and Animals Match & Discussion)

OBJECTIVE: Help children learn about Noah and how he obeyed the Lord by building an ark and how difficult it was to build and ark large enough for his family and the animals and how hard it was to gather two of every kind of animal to fill the ark. He obeyed God and was blessed with safety and peace. Those who did not obey the prophet were not blessed (drowning in the flood). See Genesis 6:17-18; 7:5).

TO MAKE VISUALS:
Copy, color, and cut out the ark and animals that follow (making two copies of each animal). Mount ark on a poster and laminate the entire poster and the animals. Have double-stick tape available to use when mounting the animals on the ark.

ACTIVITY:

1. *Match Animals.* Have children find animals (one on the left side of the room and the other on the right). Mount these on the board or walls. Have each child make their animal sounds and find the animal that matches theirs. Then one by one, the pairs can place their animals on the ark together.

2. Talk to children about how God asked Noah to build an ark and the details of building such a magnificent ship to hold his family and the animals. Talk about how those who chose not to believe the prophet Noah when he told them the earth would be flooded. They laughed at him and would not help. Then when the rains came and Noah and his family and the animals were safely inside, those who mocked Noah were drowned. After raining forty days and nights, it was safe for Noah and his family and two of every kind of animal to start a new life.

3. *Name That Commandment and Blessing.* Have the two who came up and placed their animal on the ark (one pair at a time) find their animal. Have the first name a way they can obey Heavenly Father's commandments or the prophet. Then have the second child name a blessing that comes from obeying that commandment. Then the pair can make their animal sound again and mount the animals back on the ark.

Noah

← Cut carefully along inside of dotted line. ←

chose to
be obedient.

Make 2 copies.

March—Theme 3: Living Prophets
Teach Me to Choose the Right

O, remember, my son, and learn wisdom in thy youth; yea, learn in thy youth to keep the commandments of God.

Alma 37:35

Practice Time:
Scripture Memorization—Alma

37:35 (shown left). Poster/cards (shown) are only available to download from gospelgrabbag.com.

Practice Song — Sing "Stand for the

Right" (*Children's Songbook*, 159) using the song visuals (shown right). These are only available to download from gospelgrabbag.com.

STAND FOR THE RIGHT

SHARING TIME, Week 1: **God Speaks through Living Prophets**
Activity: The Prophet Speaks
(Choice Cube)

OBJECTIVE: Help children learn WHY it is important to listen to the prophet, WHAT happens if they disobey the prophet, and HOW they are blessed by listening to and obeying the prophet.

TO MAKE VISUALS:
Copy, color, and cut out the prophet podium, commandment cards, and choice cube that follow. To make the choice cube (shown), fold box and glue together, stuff with cotton balls, and seal it with glue or tape.

ACTIVITY:
1. Ask children, "Who should we follow to know what Heavenly Father wants us to do?" Show the prophet on the podium and talk about how we can actually see and hear a real prophet today—President Thomas S. Monson, who talks to God to learn of His plan for us today. God also inspires his counselors and leaders to guide us.

2. Show children the **CHOICE CUBE** and talk about the various sides of the cube: **HOW am I blessed? WHY is this important? WHAT happens if I don't obey?**

3. Have children take turns drawing a commandment (e.g., PRAY OFTEN) that the prophet has told us God wants us to obey, and post it next to the prophet. Then have that child read it and roll the CHOICE CUBE to see which question to answer. Have them say HOW, WHY, WHAT about the commandment, answering the question relating to that commandment. Example, if they drew a PRAY OFTEN and rolled a WHY is this important?" on the cube, they might say, "Because this way I can stay close to Heavenly Father and receive His inspiration and guidance."

Why is this important?

How am I blessed?

Why is this important?

What happens if I disobey?

How am I blessed?

What happens if I disobey?

March—Theme 3: Living Prophets
Teach Me to Choose the Right

Practice Time Activities to download from gospelgrabbag.com (shown on p. 15):
Scripture to Memorize—**Alma 37:35** Posters/cards
. *Practice Song*—Sing **"Stand for the Right"** (*Children's Songbook*, 159) using song visuals .

SHARING TIME, Week 4: **I Am Blessed When I Choose to Follow the Prophet**
Activity: Obedience Brings Blessings (Stories & Testimonies)

OBJECTIVE: With these three stories, children can learn how blessings can come from obeying the prophet. Then children can have a testimony meeting to share ways they have been blessed by obeying the prophet.

TO MAKE VISUALS:
Copy, color, and cut out the images that follow for the three stories. Mount visuals on wooden craft sticks as shown (left to right): Moses and the Fiery Serpents, Nephi and the Brass Plates, Elijah and the Widow of Zarephath (oil & grain). Mount the words that follow on the back of the visuals.

ACTIVITY:
1. **SONG:** Sing the second verse of "Follow the Prophet," (*Children's Songbook*, 110-111): "*Enoc was a prophet,*" and discuss how he taught his people what was good and the people did what they should. When they became so righteous that there was no sin, Heavenly Father took the whole city up to heaven to live with Him. Talk about how we too can go back to live with Heavenly Father again if we obey His commandments.
2. **STORIES:** Ahead of time, have children learn the stories and present them to the other children, or have the leader present them.
3. **SUMMARY:** Talk to children about the stories (shown above, left to right): (1) Our prophet today, like the prophet Moses, can lead us away from the temptations and the evils attacking us. If we look to Christ (like the brass serpent) and obey God's commandments, we are blessed. (2) If Nephi and his brothers did not do as the prophet Lehi said and did not obtained the brass plates, the history of their ancestors and the words of God through prophets would have been lost forever. (3) The Widow of Zarephath had faith in the prophet and did not go hungry.
4. **TESTIMONY MEETING:** Children can share ways they have been blessed by following the prophet.

STORIES to mount on visuals:

ELIJAH AND THE WIDOW OF ZAREPHATH

Elijah was an Old Testament prophet. He was directed by the Lord to help the widow of Zarephath, whom he met gathering sticks. He asked her for water and a piece of bread. It was during a famine, and the widow had little grain and oil left. She said she had only enough to make one more loaf of bread and then she and her son would die of starvation. The prophet tested her faith and, hoping to ease her mind, said, "Fear not; go and do as thou hast said: but make me thereof a little cake [bread] first, and bring it unto me, and after make [bread] for thee and for thy son." Then he promised her she would have enough meal and oil for her and her son to eat. She did this, and there was enough to make meals until the famine ended. (1 Kings 17:8-16)

MOSES AND THE FIERY SERPENTS

As the Israelites journeyed toward the promised land, the Israelites were without bread and water and spoke against God and against Moses. The Lord sent fiery serpents. Many people were bitten by the serpents and died. Seeing the terrible destruction, the Israelites repented and asked Moses to pray for the Lord to take away the serpents and heal the people. The Lord told Moses to make a brass serpent (symbolic of Christ) and put it on a staff. Then Moses promised that anyone who had been bitten by a serpent could look at the brass serpent and they would live. The prophet Alma tells us that "there were many who were so hardened that they would not look, therefore they perished. Now the reason they would not look is because they did not believe that it would heal them" (Numbers 21:5-9; Alma 33:20).

NEPHI AND THE BRASS PLATES

After leaving Jerusalem, Lehi told Nephi that God said to take Sam, Laman, and Lemuel back to Jerusalem to get the brass plates. The plates were a history of Lehi's ancestors and words of God through His prophets.

First Laman asked the wicked Laban for the plates, but Laban tried to kill him. Laman escaped, afraid to try again. Then Nephi said to gather their gold and silver to trade for the plates, but Laban wanted it all for himself, kept the treasures, and told his servants to kill the brothers. They ran from Laban's men, and an angel told them to return unafraid.

Nephi went to Laban's house and saw him lying drunk outside. The Holy Ghost told Nephi to kill Laban with Laban's sword. Nephi didn't want to, but he was told that future generations might perish without the gospel record. Nephi obeyed, killing Laban, and then dressed in his clothes. God helped Nephi look and talk like Laban so Laban's servant would give him the plates (see 1 Nephi 3-4; 5: 21-22).

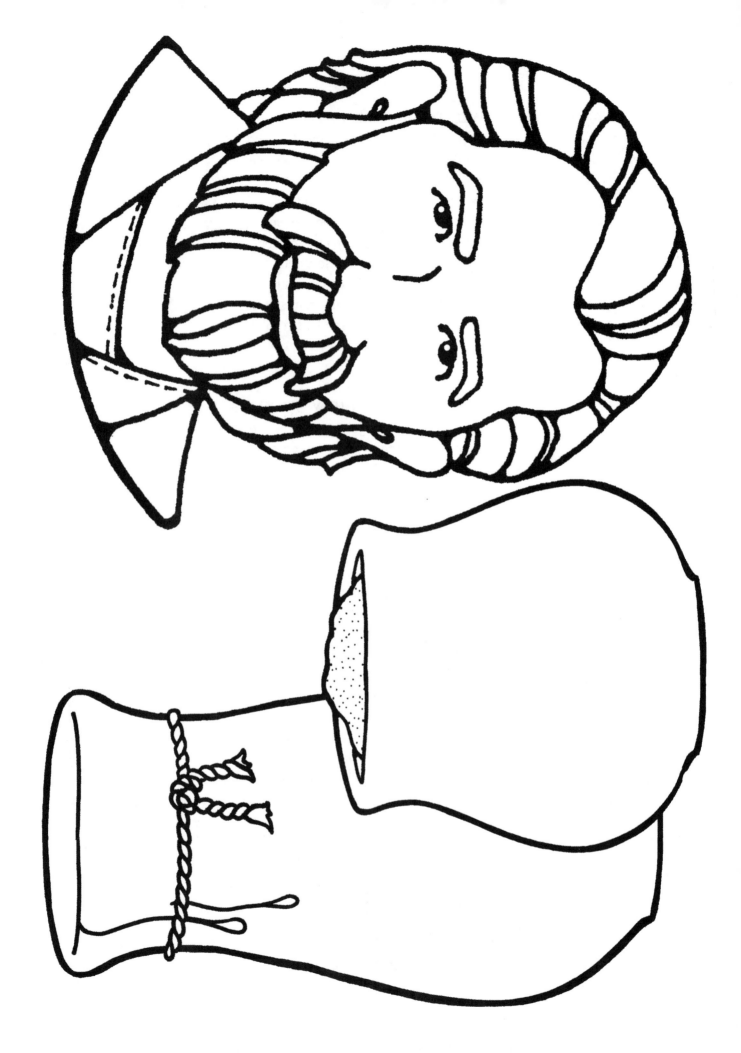

April—Theme 4: Jesus Christ Teaches Me to Choose the Right

Practice Time Activities to download from gospelgrabbag.com (shown on p. 28):

. *Scripture Memorization*—John 13:15 Posters/cards

. *Practice Song*—Sing "If the Savior Stood Beside Me" (*Friend*, Oct. 1993) and

"I Feel My Savior's Love," (*Children's Songbook*, 74) using song visuals

---

SHARING TIME, Week 4: **Jesus Christ Teaches Me to Choose the Right**
Activity: Jesus Is My Example
(I Will Follow Him Puzzle)

OBJECTIVE: Help children learn the stories of Jesus so they will know what He did and how they can follow His example.

TO MAKE: Print, color, and cut out the images that follow. Use tape or magnets to mount visuals. Mount the stories on the backs of the puzzle pieces.

ACTIVITY:

1. Randomly place the puzzle pieces—pictures of Jesus—around the board with the sign "Because I believe in Jesus Christ, I will follow Him" in the center of the board.

2. Have children take turns choosing a puzzle piece and reading the story on the back. Then tell how they can follow Jesus's example and be like Him (found after the story). Place the puzzle pieces around the sign, making them fit (as shown).

Because I believe in Jesus Christ,

Cut carefully along the inside of the dotted line.

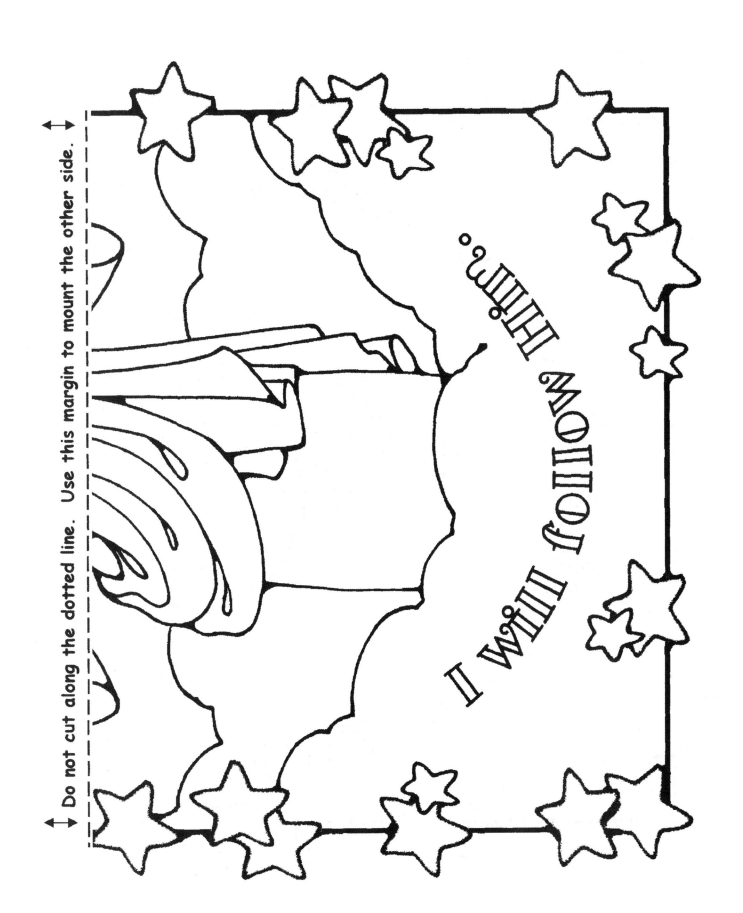

Do not cut along the dotted line.   Use this margin to mount the other side.

I will follow Him.

STORIES for "I Will Follow Him" Puzzle

JESUS LEARNED THE GOSPEL AS A BOY: When Jesus was a boy, He learned many things by reading the scriptures and praying to Heavenly Father. At age twelve, He went with Joseph and Mary into Jerusalem. When it was time to return home, Mary and Joseph had already left, thinking Jesus was with His friends. When they found that He was not, they were worried and went back to Jerusalem. They found Him in the temple talking to the wise teachers. To their surprise, Jesus knew the answers to their important gospel questions. He told His parents that He was there doing His Father's work. Jesus was helping Heavenly Father by teaching the gospel and being a missionary. (Luke 2) **I WILL FOLLOW JESUS AND TEACH THE GOSPEL TO OTHERS.**

JESUS PREPARED FOR HIS MISSION: Jesus went into the wilderness to be with God and to prepare for His mission. He stayed there for forty days. He fasted, going without eating or drinking anything. After forty days, Satan tried to tempt Jesus three times. Satan asked Jesus to jump off the temple to prove that He is God and said the angels would catch Him. Jesus said not to tempt Him. Satan wanted Jesus to turn stones into bread, but Jesus would not, even though He was hungry. Satan told Him He could have all the kingdoms and money if He would do as Satan said. After listening to the temptations, Jesus said no and told Satan to go away. (Matt. 4) **I CAN RESIST TEMPTATION LIKE JESUS DID.**

JESUS TAUGHT OTHERS TO PRAY: Jesus taught His disciples (Apostles) and others how to pray. Jesus told the people they should not pray in the streets, where others could see them. They should pray where they could be alone. He said some people pray by saying the same words over and over and that we should think about what we say. We should begin our prayers by saying, "Our Father . . . in Heaven," then thank Heavenly Father, and then ask Heavenly Father for help. Then say, "Amen." Heavenly Father will answer our prayers and bless us. (Luke 11) **I CAN PRAY TO HEAVENLY FATHER LIKE JESUS.**

JESUS WAS BAPTIZED: John the Baptist lived in the desert for many years, teaching the people about Jesus Christ. He said Jesus would come and start His church. He told the people to repent of their sins and be baptized. He said Jesus would give the Holy Ghost to them when He came. He told the people Jesus was the Savior. Jesus came to John one day while he was baptizing people in the Jordan River. Jesus asked John to baptize Him. John said Jesus did not need to be baptized because He was righteous and did not sin. Jesus told John to baptize Him and that God commanded all people to be baptized. Jesus was then baptized so He could obey all of God's commandments. When Jesus came out of the water, the Holy Ghost came to Him, and then God spoke from heaven, saying, "This is my beloved Son." (Matt. 3, Luke 3, 2 Nephi 31) **I CAN BE BAPTIZED LIKE JESUS.**

JESUS LOVED THE LITTLE CHILDREN: When Jesus was with His disciples, some people asked Him to bless their children. The disciples knew Jesus was very tired and asked the people not to bring their children to Him. Jesus loved the little children and wanted to see them. He asked His disciples to bring the children to Him. Then He blessed the children and let them know He loved them. The children loved Jesus very much. Jesus told His disciples that we should have faith like little children and then we could live with God in heaven. (Mark 10:13–15)

I WILL BE KIND AND LOVE OTHERS LIKE JESUS.

JESUS RAISED LAZARUS FROM THE DEAD: A man named Lazarus lived in Bethany with his sisters, Mary and Martha. They all loved Jesus very much. One day while Jesus was away teaching in another town, Lazarus became sick. Jesus was asked to go heal him. By the time Jesus got there, Lazarus had been dead for four days. Jesus asked Martha to believe in Him and told her Lazarus would live again. Martha told Jesus that she believed. She knew Jesus was the Savior. Mary and many others followed Jesus, crying. At the cave where Lazarus was buried, Jesus asked them to remove the stone. Jesus prayed to Heavenly Father and then spoke in a loud voice, telling Lazarus to come out of the cave. Through the power of the priesthood Jesus held, Lazarus came out alive! The people saw the miracle and knew Jesus was the Savior. (John 11) **I WILL HAVE FAITH IN THE PRIESTHOOD POWER THAT HELPED JESUS HEAL OTHERS.**

JESUS SUFFERED IN THE GARDEN: Jesus and some of His Apostles went to the Garden of Gethsemane. Jesus left them to pray, knowing He would soon need to suffer for the sins of all the people who would repent. Jesus didn't want to suffer, but He wanted to obey Heavenly Father and show His great love for us. Someone needed to pay the price for our sins. Jesus was suffering great pain when an angel came to Him to strengthen Him so He could complete what He needed to do. He was sad for all the sins of the world. His whole body shook and hurt as He bled and suffered for the sins of all men. (Matt. 26:36; Mark 14:32–42) **I WILL REPENT OF MY SINS AND FOLLOW JESUS.**

JESUS USED HIS PRIESTHOOD: One day Jesus and His disciples (Apostles) were in a boat on the Sea of Galilee. Jesus fell asleep, and the wind began to blow high waves onto the boat, filling it with water. The disciples were afraid the boat would sink, so they awoke Jesus, asking Him for help. Jesus stood, commanded the wind to stop blowing, and told the waves to go down. Jesus asked the Apostles why they were afraid and told them they should have more faith. (Mark 4:35–40) **I WILL HAVE FAITH LIKE JESUS.**

May—Theme 5:
I Choose the Right When I Am Baptized and Confirmed a Member of the Church

Repent, and be baptized every one of you in the name of Jesus Christ for the remission of sins, and ye shall receive the gift of the Holy Ghost.

Acts 2:38

Practice Time:
Scripture Memorization—Acts 2:38
(shown left). Poster/cards (shown) are only available to download from gospelgrabbag.com.

Practice Song—Sing "When I Am Baptized" (*Children's Songbook*, 103) (shown right), and **"Baptism"** (*CS*, 100), and **"When Jesus Was Baptized"** (*CS*, 102) using the song visuals. These are only available to download from gospelgrabbag.com.

WHEN I AM BAPTIZED

SHARING TIME, Week 1: **As I Repent, I Can Be Forgiven**
Activity: Eraser Promises
(Steps-to-Repentance Pencil and Bookmark)

Objective: Help children learn the steps of repentance so they can erase the wrong by receiving forgiveness and making right choices.

TO MAKE: Print, color, and cut out the images and stories that follow in cardstock, as well as a bookmark for each child. Mount the wordstrips on the backs of the pencil parts. Place double-stick tape on the back of the pencil parts and eraser, or use magnets to mount them on the board.

44

ACTIVITY:

Tell the scripture story of Alma the Younger and the sons of Mosiah (Mosiah 27:8, 10, 32, 34-35).

Part 1: Review repentance steps as you show parts 1-6 on the pencil (read D&C 58:42-43). Heavenly Father has promised us that if we repent, He will erase our sin(s) and He will "remember them no more."

Part 2:

1. Take the pencil apart, placing pieces around the board, and leave a space to reassemble the pencil.
2. Tell Nathan's story (see REPENTANCE STORY #1 on the story page—included with the patterns).
3. Talk about the steps of repentance (found on the pencil, shown), telling how Nathan took the toys back to Carson and what he did to repent.
4. Choose several children to come up and put the pencil together to show the steps of repentance.

Part 3:

1. Give each class teacher a repentance story (use REPENTANCE STORIES 2-7 on the following page). Each story talks about a wrong choice that requires repentance. If playing the game as a family, pair off in twos, placing a teen or adult with each child. Ask the children in the group to decide what needs to be done to right the wrong and repent.
2. Have children tell the steps of repentance (found on the pencil) and what the characters in the stories should do to repent.
3. Encourage children to read stories in the scriptures where others repented and erased their sin.

    BOOKMARK: Children can enjoy this bookmark reminder of the 6 steps to repentance.

STORIES:

REPENTANCE STORY #1: Nathan and Carson were best friends and had fun playing at Carson's house. Nathan liked Carson's toys and wished they were his. Nathan decided to borrow some of Carson's toys and put them in his backpack without asking. Later, at his house that night, Nathan played with the toys, but it wasn't much fun. His dad asked him why he was unhappy. Nathan said he borrowed Carson's toys without asking and he felt bad. Nathan's dad told him it was wrong to take something that belonged to someone else. He asked Nathan to decide what he should do to right the wrong. Nathan took the toys back and told Carson he was sorry. Nathan promised never to do it again. Carson was happy his friend was honest.   **WHAT CAN NATHAN DO TO REPENT?**

Continued . . .

REPENTANCE STORY #2: Darren wanted to ride his bike to the store with his friend Jeff. His mother told him not to take the narrow road because it wasn't safe. Darren decided to take the narrow road anyway to show Jeff how brave he was. As they were picking up speed, Darren's bike hit a rock, and he accidently ran into Jeff's bike. This pushed Jeff off the path into a passing car. He was rushed to the hospital. Jeff suffered a broken arm and leg.   **WHAT CAN DARREN DO TO REPENT?**

REPENTANCE STORY #3: Nicky and her brother Josh liked to go into the gully. There were lots lizards, bugs, and trees, and a creek with running water where they often found fish. One day they went into the gully to catch some fish. Before they went, they were playing ball with the younger neighbor children and decided to take them along. They thought they would be right back, so they didn't ask their parents. It took them longer than they thought to get there. It was getting dark, and they were still not home. The parents of the children became worried. They called the police to search for them. When the children came home, their mothers were crying on the front porch. Nicky and Josh had no idea how much pain they had caused.   **WHAT CAN NICKY AND JOSH DO TO REPENT?**

REPENTANCE STORY #4: Trisha and her friend Tess liked to play each day. They didn't like playing with anyone else. At Primary, they sat together and talked and giggled. They often talked while the Primary leaders were giving Sharing Time. They didn't sing when it was time; they just talked. A new girl came to their class and sat next to Trisha. Tess came in and asked her to move so she could sit by Trisha. They didn't say hi or try to talk to the new girl; they just talked to each other and giggled. The next week, the new girl didn't come to Primary. The teacher was worried and went to see the new girl. The girl said she didn't feel like she had any friends.   **WHAT CAN TRISHA AND TESS DO TO REPENT?**

REPENTANCE STORY #5: Jenny and Emily liked to go to Primary Activity Days during the week. They had fun at the activities. Each time they passed Wendy's house, they thought about asking her to go, but they never invited her. Wendy was not a member of the Church and didn't have many friends. She would have gone with them every week, but she was never asked. **WHAT CAN JENNY AND EMILY DO TO REPENT?**

REPENTANCE STORY #6: Pat liked to make wooden cars. He learned how to carve them in Scouts. His dad helped him build the best car. He bragged that his car would move faster than the others in the Pinewood Derby. They placed their cars at the top of the hill and watched them raced down. Nathan, another Scout, had tried to build the best car that he could, but his dad worked long hours and came home after Nathan was in bed. Nathan's car was okay, but it didn't have the right curves in the back to make it move as fast as Pat's. Pat's car won, and he bragged about his dad helping him. Nathan went home feeling bad.   **WHAT CAN PAT DO TO REPENT?**

REPENTANCE STORY #7: Clay and his friend Ben walked to school together each day. They passed by some boys who teased them every day and called them names. Ben and Clay wanted to protect themselves in case the boys started a fight. They filled their pockets with rocks so they would be ready. The next day the mean boys came at them, and Clay pulled a rock out of his pocket and threw it at one of the boys. It hit his ear, and the boy began to cry. When they got to school, the injured boy had to go to the doctor.   **WHAT CAN CLAY AND BEN DO TO REPENT?**

Eraser Promise:

"Behold, he who has repented of his sins, the same is forgiven, and I, the Lord, remember them no more." —D&C 58:42

Gospelgrabbag.com

1 Recognize I've done something wrong.

2 Promise not to do it again.

3 Do all I can to correct what I did wrong and apologize to those I have offended.

4 Pray to my Heavenly Father for forgiveness.

5 Promise to live the commandments to find joy.

6 Forgive myself.

Bookmark (repeated three times)

Eraser Promise:
"Behold, he who has repented of his sins, the same is forgiven, and I, the Lord, remember them no more." -D&C 58:42

6 Forgive myself.

5 Promise to live the commandments to find joy.

4 Pray to my Heavenly Father for forgiveness.

3 apologize to those I have offended.

Do all I can to correct what I did wrong and

2 Promise not to do it again.

1 Recognize I've done something wrong.

©JKing

I know how to repent!

Eraser Promise:
"Behold, he who has repented of his sins, the same is forgiven, and I, the Lord, remember them no more." -D&C 58:42

6 Forgive myself.

5 Promise to live the commandments to find joy.

4 Pray to my Heavenly Father for forgiveness.

3 apologize to those I have offended.

Do all I can to correct what I did wrong and

2 Promise not to do it again.

1 Recognize I've done something wrong.

©JKing

I know how to repent!

Eraser Promise:
"Behold, he who has repented of his sins, the same is forgiven, and I, the Lord, remember them no more." -D&C 58:42

6 Forgive myself.

5 Promise to live the commandments to find joy.

4 Pray to my Heavenly Father for forgiveness.

3 apologize to those I have offended.

Do all I can to correct what I did wrong and

2 Promise not to do it again.

1 Recognize I've done something wrong.

©JKing

I know how to repent!

May–Theme 5: I Choose the Right When I am Baptized and Confirmed a Member of the Church

Practice Time Activities to download from gospelgrabbag.com (shown on p. 44):

. *Scripture Memorization*—Acts 2:38 Posters/cards

. *Practice Song*—Sing **"When I Am Baptized"** (Children's Songbook, 103), **"Baptism"** (CS, 100), and **"When Jesus Was Baptized"** (CS, 102) using song visuals

SHARING TIME, Week 3: **The Holy Ghost Can Help Me**
Activity: Tune into the Holy Ghost
(Inspiration Station Concentration)

OBJECTIVE:

Help children learn six ways the Holy Ghost helps us: teach us, comfort us, testify of Jesus Christ, tell us what to do or not to do, and help us do good.

TO MAKE VISUALS:

Copy, color, and cut out the radio and cards as follows. You will need two copies of each card (follow directions on how many to copy of each sheet). Mount the radio in the center of a poster as shown and laminate the entire poster. Mount each card, showing how the Holy Ghost helps us on the back of each Inspiration Station card. Laminate cards.

ACTIVITY:

1. Ahead of time, mix up and post the cards facedown with double-stick tape with the Inspiration Station sides facing up. Place double-stick tape on the Inspiration Station side of the card so it will be ready to mount when you play the game.

2. Showing the poster with the cards, tell the children, "The radio we have in our car or home transmits music and words we can hear with our ears. The Holy Ghost has a power given to Him by Heavenly Father to transmit messages to our minds and hearts to help us choose the right."

3. Tell the children, "If we tune into Inspiration Station (pointing to the radio knob and the Inspiration Station cards), we can receive messages from the Holy Ghost that teach us, comfort us, testify of Jesus Christ, tell us what to do or not to do, and help us do good." (You could show these cards as you talk about them—then place them randomly in another spot facedown before playing.)

4. Ask the children, "What can we do to be worthy of the Holy Ghost's guidance?" Choose the right each day. We don't want static by making wrong decisions. We want to be able to hear the Spirit's messages clearly. "What are other ways we can tune into His Spirit?" When we pray, read the scriptures, and listen with our hearts and minds.

5. Say, "Let's play this Inspiration Station Concentration game to learn how the Holy Ghost inspires us."

To Play: Have the children take turns turning two cards over to make a match.

Sharing Testimonies: Ahead of time, give out six of the "Holy Ghost" cards (shown right) to six different children and ask them to talk about how the Holy Ghost has helped them (relating to the card). Example: For the card **"The Holy Ghost will comfort us,"** the child might say, "When I was afraid to go to sleep, I prayed, and I felt a peaceful, comforting feeling."

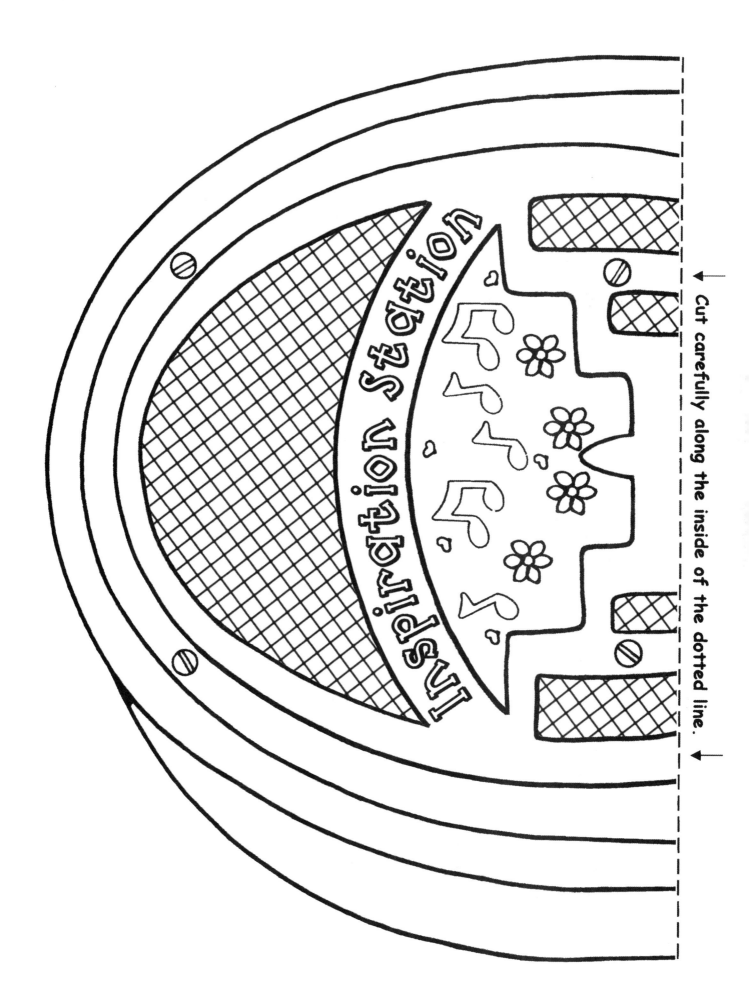

Inspiration Station

Cut carefully along the inside of the dotted line.

Intune Radio

Do not cut along the dotted line. Use this margin to mount the other side.

The Holy Ghost will teach us

The Holy Ghost will comfort us

The Holy Ghost will testify of Jesus Christ

The Holy Ghost will tell us what to do or not do

The Holy Ghost will help us do good

The Holy Ghost will warn us of danger

June—Theme 6:
I Choose the Right by Living Gospel Principles

I will go and do the things which the Lord hath commanded, for I know that the Lord giveth no commandments unto the children of men, save he shall prepare a way for them that they may accomplish the thing which he commandeth them.

1 Nephi 3:7

Practice Time:
Scripture Memorization—
1 Nephi 3:7 (shown left). Poster/cards (shown) are only available to <u>download from gospelgrabbag.com</u>.

*Practice Song—*Sing "Nephi's **Courage**" (*Children's Songbook*, 120-121) using the song visuals (shown right). These are only available to <u>download from gospelgrabbag.com</u>.

NEPHI'S COURAGE

SHARING TIME, Week 2: **When I Pay My Tithing, Heavenly Father Will Bless Me**
Activity: Open the Windows of Heaven

OBJECTIVE: Children will learn that if they pay their tithing, the windows of heaven will open and Heavenly Father will pour out blessings (Malachi 3:10). They will learn where their tithing money goes and the blessings it brings.

TO MAKE VISUALS: Copy, color, and cut out windows (five copies) and pictures and clue cards that follow. Laminate images. Mount pictures on a poster and laminate the entire poster. Cut windows on lines around window, folding so windows can open to pictures. Then mount windows over pictures so window flap opens. Place tithing clue cards in a container to draw from, and have double-stick tape ready to mount cards on posters.

ACTIVITY:
Tell children, "Heavenly Father has given us many great blessings, and He asks us to pay only one tenth of all we earn to build up the kingdom of God upon the earth." Tell the following story of how the windows of heaven can be opened because of paying tithing.

Story: Lorenzo Snow, a latter-day prophet, was concerned that the Church and its members were in debt and needed help. He prayed about this problem. He was inspired to go to St. George, where the Saints were suffering from a severe drought. They were praying for rain to water their crops so they would have food to eat. While there, the prophet prayed and received an answer to the promise found in Malachi 3:8–12, that if they paid their tithing, the "windows of heaven" would be opened and they would receive so many blessings there would not be enough room to receive them. They would be blessed both temporally (receive rain to water their crops) and spiritually (increase their faith and testimony). The Saints paid their tithing and the rains came—really "pouring out blessings." We too can have the same type of blessings as we keep the law of tithing.

Windows of Heaven Review:
Ask children, "Do you know how Heavenly Father and Jesus want us—the Church—to use our tithing money? Open each window of heaven and talk about the pictures and the descriptions that follow to review. Say, "Our tithing money goes to (look for codes on cards: BT, BC, E, FH, MP):

BUILD TEMPLES to seal families together forever and help ancestors receive their temple ordinances. **BT**
BUILD CHURCHES so we can learn about the gospel, take the sacrament, and worship. **BC**
EDUCATE in church schools, seminaries, and institutes. To prepare, print, and send lesson materials to teach members all around the world. **E**
FAMILY HISTORY information and records can be gathered to help find our ancestors; then temple work can be done. **FH**
MISSIONARY PROGRAM to help preach the gospel to everyone in the world. **MP**

Clue Match Game: Divide children into teams to play, and take turns drawing a card and reading it aloud. Then place it under the window it matches (opening the windows to find it). For example, if they draw the card that reads, "Tithing helps families become forever families," then the child will find the window with the temple and place the card under this window to show that our tithing will BUILD TEMPLES.

Do not cut along the dotted line. Use this margin to mount the other side.

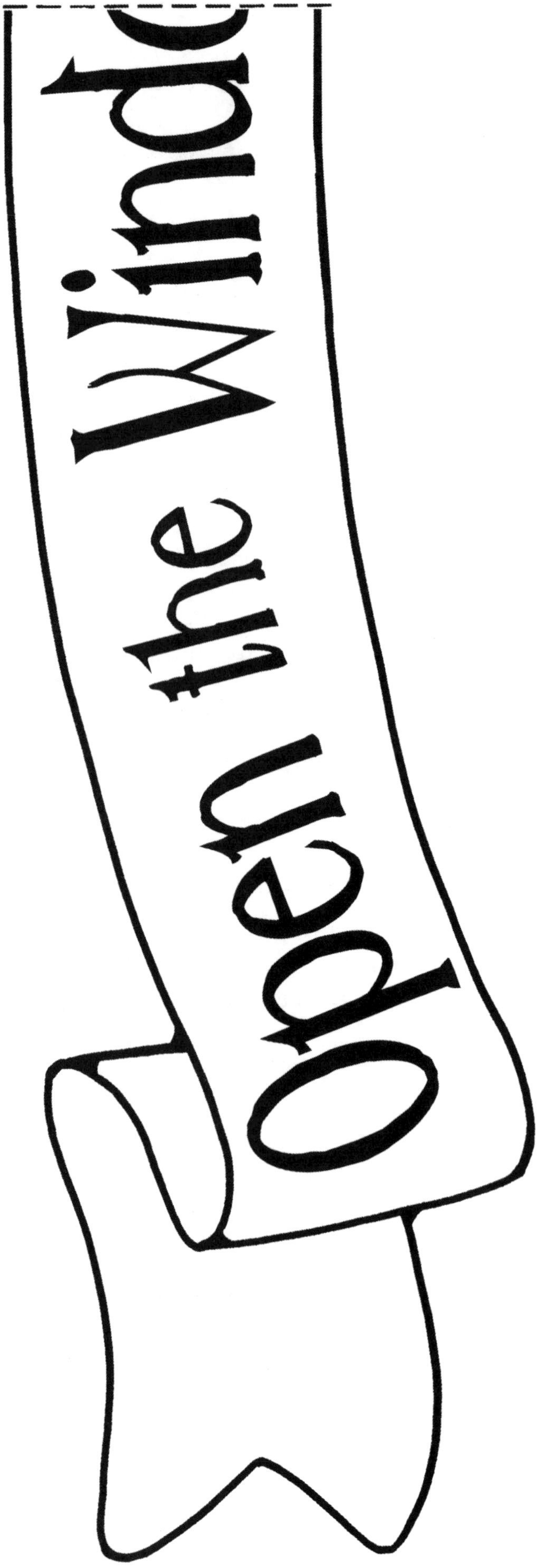

Open the Wind○

ows of Heaven

Cut carefully along the inside of the dotted line.

Make 5 copies.

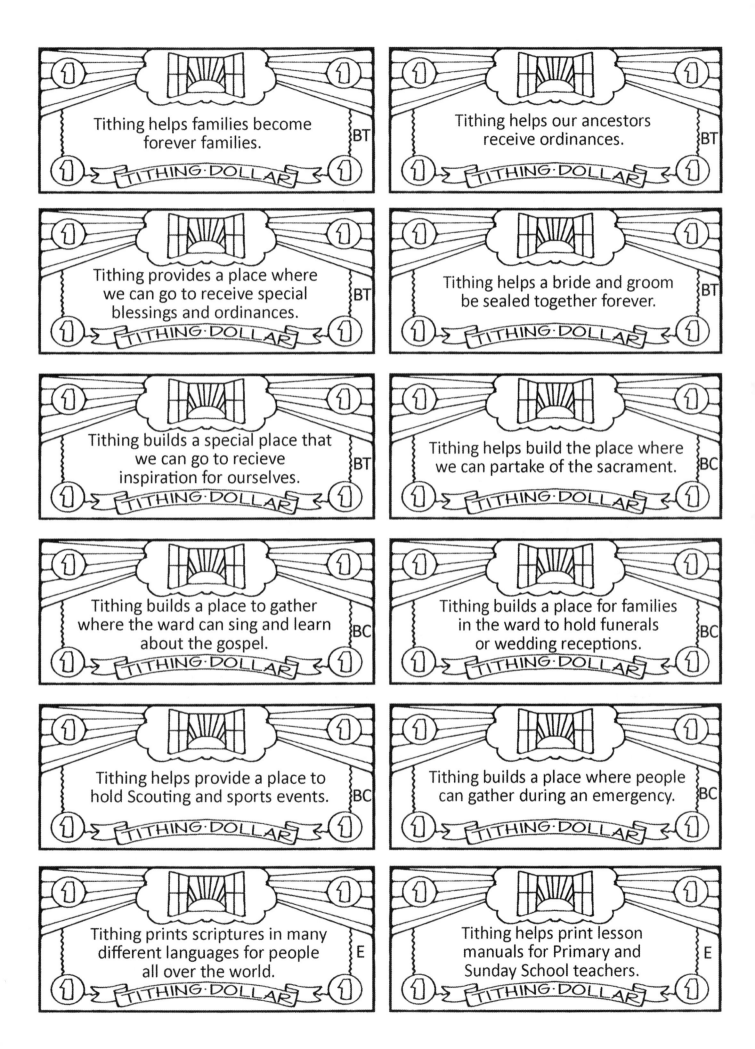

Tithing helps families become forever families. **BT**

Tithing helps our ancestors receive ordinances. **BT**

Tithing provides a place where we can go to receive special blessings and ordinances. **BT**

Tithing helps a bride and groom be sealed together forever. **BT**

Tithing builds a special place that we can go to recieve inspiration for ourselves. **BT**

Tithing helps build the place where we can partake of the sacrament. **BC**

Tithing builds a place to gather where the ward can sing and learn about the gospel. **BC**

Tithing builds a place for families in the ward to hold funerals or wedding receptions. **BC**

Tithing helps provide a place to hold Scouting and sports events. **BC**

Tithing builds a place where people can gather during an emergency. **BC**

Tithing prints scriptures in many different languages for people all over the world. **E**

Tithing helps print lesson manuals for Primary and Sunday School teachers. **E**

TITHING·DOLLAR

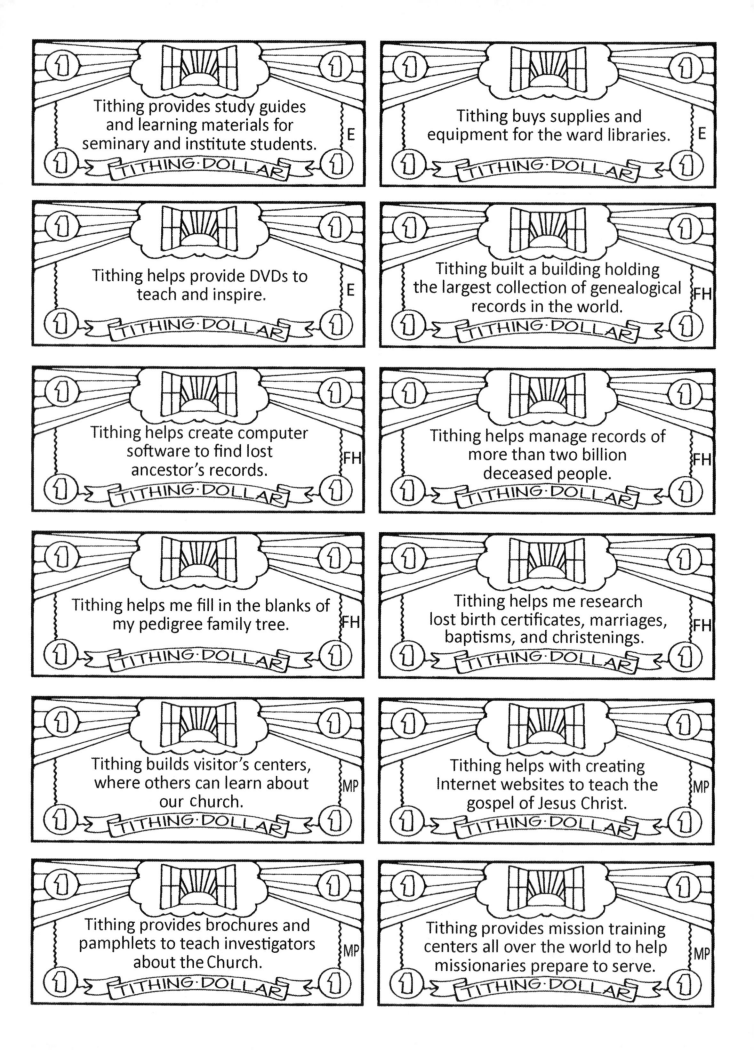

Tithing provides study guides and learning materials for seminary and institute students. E

Tithing buys supplies and equipment for the ward libraries. E

Tithing helps provide DVDs to teach and inspire. E

Tithing built a building holding the largest collection of genealogical records in the world. FH

Tithing helps create computer software to find lost ancestor's records. FH

Tithing helps manage records of more than two billion deceased people. FH

Tithing helps me fill in the blanks of my pedigree family tree. FH

Tithing helps me research lost birth certificates, marriages, baptisms, and christenings. FH

Tithing builds visitor's centers, where others can learn about our church. MP

Tithing helps with creating Internet websites to teach the gospel of Jesus Christ. MP

Tithing provides brochures and pamphlets to teach investigators about the Church. MP

Tithing provides mission training centers all over the world to help missionaries prepare to serve. MP

TITHING·DOLLAR

June—Theme 6: I Choose the Right by Living Gospel Principles

Practice Time Activities to download from gospelgrabbag.com (shown on p. 59):
. *Scripture Memorization* — 1 **Nephi 3:7** Posters/cards
. *Practice Song* — Sing "*Nephi's Courage*" (*Children's Songbook, 120-121*) using song visuals

---

SHARING TIME, Week 3: *I Obey the Word of Wisdom by Eating and Drinking That Which Is Good and Avoiding That Which Is Bad*

Activity: My Body Is a Temple (Concentration)

OBJECTIVE: Help children know that they are created in the image of God and that their body is like a temple. *References: Genesis 1:27; 1 Corinthians 3:16–17; D&C 89; David A. Bednar, "Ye Are the Temple of God," Ensign, Sept. 2001.*

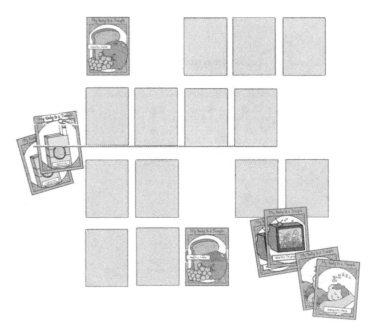

TO MAKE VISUALS:
Copy, color, and cut out the images, shown, that follow, making two sets of the game cards. Mount numbers on the back of one set and letters on the back of the other set. Then laminate and cut out. Place double-stick tape on the back of the cards.

ACTIVITY:
To Set Up: You will need two sets of cards.
Mix up cards, and place them facedown on the board.
1. Tell children that their body is like a temple because they were made in God's holy image. We are sons and daughters of Heavenly Father, and our brother is Jesus Christ. Heavenly Father and Jesus have told us that no unclean thing should enter the temple, meaning our bodies are sacred (1 Corinthians 3:16–17; Genesis 1:27).
2. Have children take turns turning two cards over to make a match, returning them to their original spots.
3. Mount matches on the board faceup, placing the SHOULD NOT dos on the left and the SHOULD dos on the right.
4. Talk about each set of choices and why they think Heavenly Father does not or does want them to partake of these things.

My Body Is a Temple

Uplifting books

My Body Is a Temple

Good thoughts

My Body Is a Temple

Coffee

My Body Is a Temple

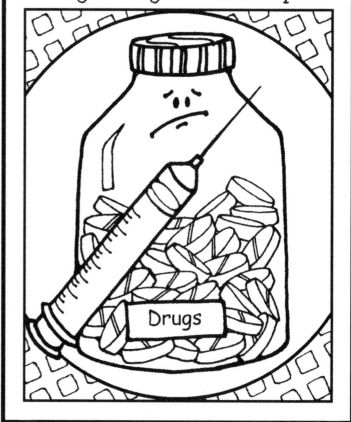

Drugs

My Body Is a Temple

Alcohol

My Body Is a Temple

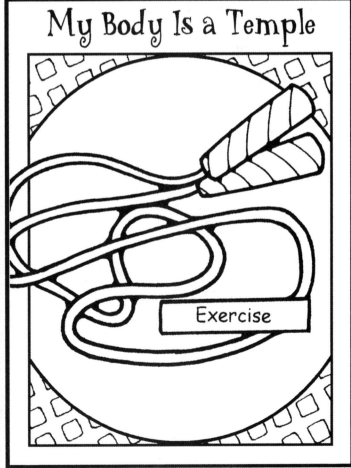

Adequate sleep

My Body Is a Temple

Healthful drinks

MILK

My Body Is a Temple

Exercise

My Body Is a Temple

Worthy TV programs

My Body Is a Temple

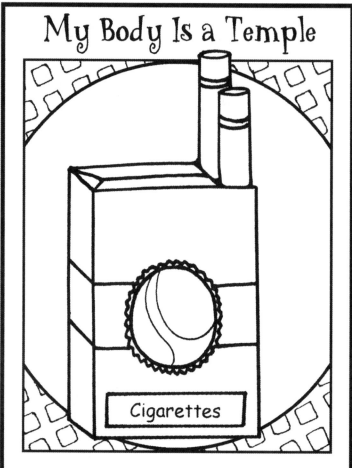

Cigarettes

My Body Is a Temple

Modest clothing

My Body Is a Temple

Healthful foods

My Body Is a Temple

Crude words

My Body Is a Temple

Kind words

My Body Is a Temple

Uplifting music

My Body Is a Temple

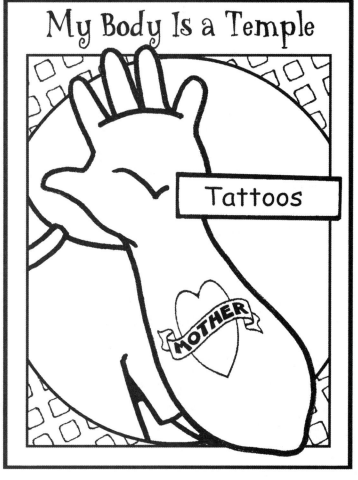

Tattoos

July—Theme 7:
I Choose the Right by Living Gospel Principles

Practice Time:
Scripture Memorization—

1 Nephi 3:16 (shown left). Poster/cards (shown) are only available to download from gospelgrabbag.com.

*Practice Song—*Sing "**The Wise Man and the Foolish Man**" (*Children's Songbook*, 281) using song visuals (shown), only available to download from gospelgrabbag.com.

USE FOR THIS MONTH'S AND/OR AUGUST'S SHARING TIME

SHARING TIME, Week 2 (July): **Being Kind and Doing and Saying Nice Things to Others**
SHARING TIME, Week 1 (August): **Having Good Friends Will Help Me Choose the Right**

Activity: FRIEND-OR-FOE? (Slap Game / Flip Games)

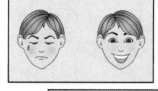

OBJECTIVE: Learn the difference between being a FRIEND and a FOE (someone who is not a friend). A FRIEND is patient, cheerful, nice, and helpful. A FOE is like an enemy; impatient, not kind, grouchy, and uncaring.

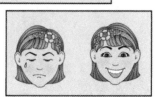

TO MAKE VISUALS: Copy, color, and cut out the girl and boy smile/frown faces and situation cards (two sets of boys and two sets of girls).
MOUNTING: (1) Mount faces as shown right creating two posters. (2) Mount the two faces front and back on paint sticks (as shown).

ACTIVITY: Give points to teams with right answers; team with most points wins!
#1 FRIEND-OR-FOE? SLAP GAME: Mount the face signs on the board, and line children up in two teams facing their signs. Leader reads the top portion of the card and then one of the actions below (without saying FRIEND or FOE). The two children compete to see who slaps the right face first. Does the action make a friend SMILE, showing they are a FRIEND, or does the action make a friend FROWN, showing they are a FOE? You could also read the other action (FRIEND or FOE) and talk about it.
#2 FRIEND-OR-FOE? FLIP GAME: Divide children into two teams, keeping them in their seats, or continue with the same teams as #1, only seated. Take turns choosing players in the teams to come up front to hold the faces on the sticks. Play the same as #1 above only now the two competing children flip their face to the correct face/answer (FRIEND smile) or FOE frown).

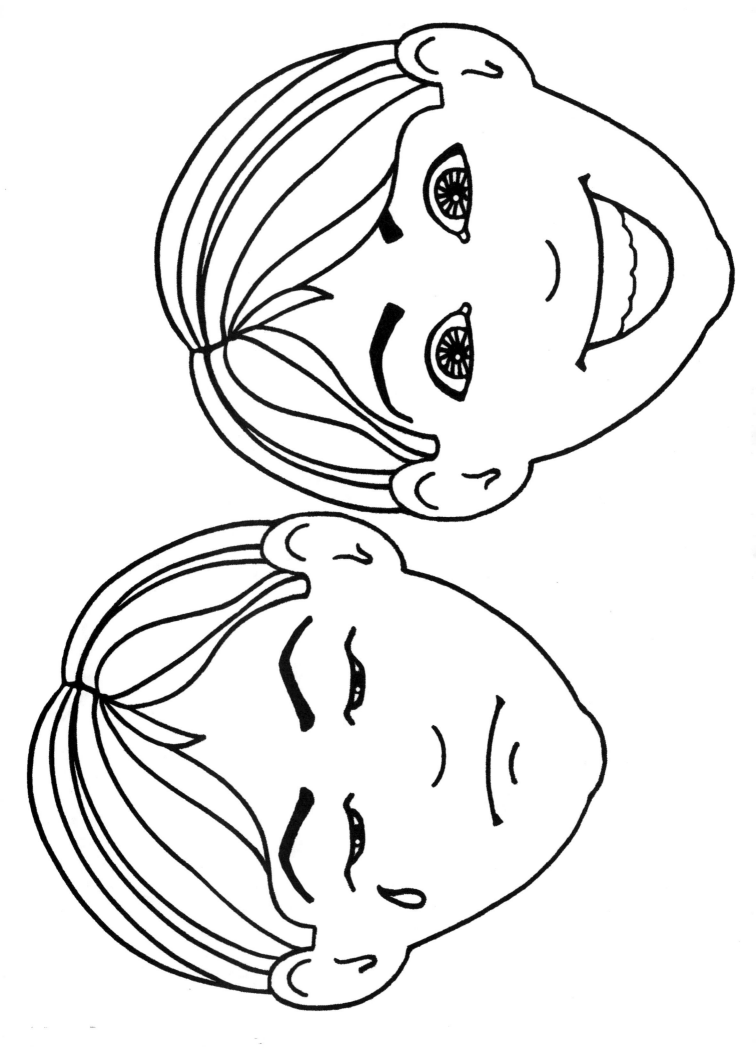

FRIEND OR FOE?

MY FRIEND was having trouble with his math, and I was good at math. So I

- - - - - - - - - - - - - - - - - - - -

(friend) . . . told him I would help him solve the problems after school.

(foe) . . . didn't offer help so I could shine bright in class.

FRIEND OR FOE?

MY FRIEND was playing a game with his grandfather when I came over to play. So I

- - - - - - - - - - - - - - - - - - - -

(foe) . . . said, "Come on, let's go; we don't have time for old people."

(friend) . . . said, "Can I play? Then maybe your grandpa can come watch us play ball."

FRIEND OR FOE?

MY FRIEND's mother forgot to pack a sandwich in his lunch box. So I

- - - - - - - - - - - - - - - - - - - -

(friend) . . . said, "Here, have half of mine."

(foe) . . . said, "You should remind her tomorrow to pack one for you; I need all of mine."

FRIEND OR FOE?

MY FRIEND's shirt got torn on the playground. So I

- - - - - - - - - - - - - - - - - - - -

(friend) . . . offered my under-T-shirt to wear the rest of the day.

(foe) . . . said, "You should go call your mom to bring you a new shirt."

FRIEND OR FOE?

MY FRIEND said he didn't know what to wear the next day for the costume party at school. So I

- - - - - - - - - - - - - - - - - - - -

(friend) . . . said to call me after school and we could invent one to wear.

(foe) . . . bragged about how cool my costume was going to be.

FRIEND OR FOE?

MY FRIEND'S dog ran away, and my friend was sad and scared that the dog would get hit by a car. So I

- - - - - - - - - - - - - - - - - - - -

(friend) . . . went out with him to look for the dog.

(foe) . . . said, "My dog got lost once, and we never found him."

FRIEND OR FOE?

MY FRIEND's grandmother was sick when I came over to play. So I

- - - - - - - - - - - - - - - - - - -

(friend) . . . said, "Let's make up a goodie bag full of things that will cheer her up."

(foe) . . . said, "You promised you could hang out with me."

FRIEND OR FOE?

MY FRIEND noticed it was getting dark outside, and he didn't know his way home. So I

- - - - - - - - - - - - - - - - - - -

(friend) . . . asked him if he wanted to go home with me, then we could give him a ride home.

(foe) . . . told him, "Scary, dude! I hope you make it!"

FRIEND OR FOE?

MY FRIEND wanted to play on our soccer team, but he really isn't a good player. So I

- - - - - - - - - - - - - - - - - - -

(friend) . . . said I would coach him after school to get him ready for the team.

(foe) . . . said, "Maybe next year you will be good enough."

FRIEND OR FOE?

MY FRIEND forgot that it was picture day today at school and wasn't ready. So I

- - - - - - - - - - - - - - - - - - -

(friend) . . . helped her fix her hair and let her wear my new top.

(foe) . . . showed off the new top my mom bought me just in time for pictures.

FRIEND OR FOE?

MY FRIEND liked to ride bikes with us, but he couldn't keep up. So I

- - - - - - - - - - - - - - - - - - -

(friend) . . . slowed down to wait for him to catch up.

(foe) . . . kept going, knowing he would be left behind.

FRIEND OR FOE?

MY FRIEND said she wanted to try out for the princess in our school play. So I

- - - - - - - - - - - - - - - - - - -

(friend) . . . helped her read the lines before the tryout so she would feel more confident.

(foe) . . . made sure I knew the lines really well so she wouldn't have a chance.

FRIEND OR FOE?

MY FRIEND was too shy to play at recess because she accidently cut her bangs too short. So I

(friend) . . . told her no one will care if her bangs were too short because she had pretty eyes.

(foe) . . . walked away, giggling and telling my friends about it.

FRIEND OR FOE?

MY FRIEND wanted to learn to ride a skateboard but didn't have one. So I

(friend) . . . asked him if he wanted to practice with me after school.

(foe) . . . said, "It's sad you're so clumsy."

FRIEND OR FOE?

MY FRIEND was sitting on her front porch with her skates, but she didn't know how to skate. So I

(friend) . . . showed her how it was done, then got my friend to take hold of her arms to steady her as she went.

(foe) . . . showed her how good I was, as I skated off.

FRIEND OR FOE?

MY FRIEND had to wear her old coat to school from last year, but it was too small. So I

(friend) . . . asked my Mom to fix the sleeves on her coat, then she found one that fit her just right.

(foe) . . . told her to ask her Mom to buy her a new one.

FRIEND OR FOE?

MY FRIEND's bike got a flat tire when it was time for us to ride home. So I

(friend) . . . walked home with him and had my dad patch it up.

(foe) . . . said I would call his dad to come and get him, leaving him behind.

FRIEND OR FOE?

MY FRIEND was still working on his chores when it was time for soccer. So I

(friend) . . . stayed and started helping so he could go.

(foe) . . . said, "Too bad you didn't get your work done in time to play."

FRIEND OR FOE?

MY FRIEND wanted ice cream but didn't bring money to buy one. So I

(friend) . . . asked the guys to to buy a double scoop for him.

(foe) . . . ate our ice cream in front of him, reminding him to bring money next time.

FRIEND OR FOE?

MY FRIEND had trouble reading his scriptures in our Primary class. So I

(friend) . . . asked the teacher if we could practice some of the scriptures for next week to read in class together.

(foe) . . . giggled with my friends saying, "The word is _____."

FRIEND OR FOE?

MY FRIEND was kicking rocks on the playground when I heard him say he didn't know anyone at school. So I

(friend) . . . told him my name and asked him to play ball with us.

(foe) . . . ignored him while having a good time with my friends.

FRIEND OR FOE?

MY FRIEND and I both brought apples for our teacher, but my friend forgot and took a bite out of hers. So I

(friend) . . . said, "Let's go give my apple to the teacher and say it is from both of us."

(foe) . . . polished my apple extra shiny before giving it to the teacher and said, "Too bad you ate yours."

FRIEND OR FOE?

MY FRIEND was crying one day at school because someone had called a terrible name. So I

(friend) . . . went over to talk to her and ask her what I could do to make her feel better.

(foe) . . . whispered to my friend that she was a cry-baby.

FRIEND OR FOE?

MY FRIEND told me he had taken some money off my dresser and wanted to return it. So I

(friend) . . . quickly forgave him and thanked him for telling me.

(foe) . . . told him I would never talk to him again and to leave.

August—Theme 8: I Choose to Fill My Life With Things That Invite the Spirit

If there is anything virtuous, lovely, or of good report or praiseworthy, we seek after these things.

Articles of Faith 1:13

Practice Time:

Scripture Memorization—Articles of Faith 1:13 (shown left). Poster/cards (shown) are only available to download from gospelgrabbag.com.

Practice Song—Sing "I'm Trying to Be like Jesus" (Children's Songbook, 78-79) using the song visuals (shown right). These are only available to download from gospelgrabbag.com.

I'M TRYING TO BE LIKE JESUS

SHARING TIME, Weeks 3 and 4:
I Should Do Things on the Sabbath That Will Help Me Stay Close to Heavenly Father

Activity: Keeping the Sabbath Holy (Sunny Sunday Activities)

OBJECTIVE: Help children understand which activities will help them keep the gospel standard "I will do the things on the Sabbath that will help me feel close to Heavenly Father and Jesus Christ" ("My Gospel Standards"). Ideas: Exodus 20:8; D&C 59:9-14; "Sabbath," *True to the Faith*, 145-147.

TO MAKE VISUALS:
Copy, color, and cut out the Sunny Sunday sun (yellow), Gloomy Glum-Day circle (blue), Gospel Standard banner, sun rays, clouds, and wordstrips. Laminate them and cut them out. Laminate a mounting poster. Mount sun, circle, and sign on poster as shown. *Note:* Do not tape or glue sun sides to poster to leave an opening where sun rays can be inserted (see Activity 1: Forecasting the Weather [step #4] that follows).

ACTIVITY 1—*Forecasting the Weather:*

1. Tell children that Sunday can be a ***Sunny Sunday*** filled with activities that help you feel close to Heavenly Father and Jesus, or it can be a ***Gloomy Glum-Day*** if you do activities that are not appropriate for the Sabbath. These activities are okay on other days, but Sunday is a special day. On Sunday, Heavenly Father wants us to rest from our labors, avoid making others work, spend time with our family, attend our Church meetings, and do things that will help us keep the gospel standard (have children repeat) "I will do the things on the Sabbath that will help me feel close to Heavenly Father and Jesus Christ."

2. Place a sun ray on the sun and say, "<u>Let's find activities that will brighten our sun, making the Sabbath a ***Sunny Sunday***.</u>" Place a cloud on the circle and say, "<u>Lets identify activities that might make us sad for not keeping the Sabbath day, making it a ***Gloomy Glum-Day***.</u>"

3. Tell children, counting on your fingers, "There are five questions we can ask to know if the activity will help us have a ***Sunny Sunday***. Does it help me: (1) think of Jesus, (2) be reverent, (3) learn the gospel, (4) spend time with family, or (5) rest?"

4. Have children help you determine what their spiritual weather would be like on Sunday by the actions they choose. Have them come up one at a time, choose a wordstrip, and read it aloud. Then have children choose a sun ray if the activity is a ***Sunny Sunday*** activity, and place the ray behind the sun (as shown). Or if it is a ***Gloomy Glum-Day*** activity, have children place the cloud on or around the circle (as shown).

ACTIVITY 2—*Sunny Side-Up Voting:* Read wordstrip/activities again and have children vote on activities. Have all children vote or have individual classes come up and vote as follows:
Option 1—With a thumbs-up if it is a ***Sunny Sunday*** activity and with a thumbs down if it is a ***Gloomy Glum-Day*** activity.
Option 2—Say "warm" for ***Sunny Sunday*** or "cold" for ***Gloomy Glum-Day*** activities.
Option 3—Smile for ***Sunny Sunday*** or frown for ***Gloomy Glum-Day*** activities.

Cut carefully along the inside of the dotted line.

Sunny · Sun

Do not cut along the dotted line. Use this margin to mount the other side.

I will do those things on the Sabbath that will help me feel close to Heavenly Father and Jesus Christ.

—My Gospel Standards

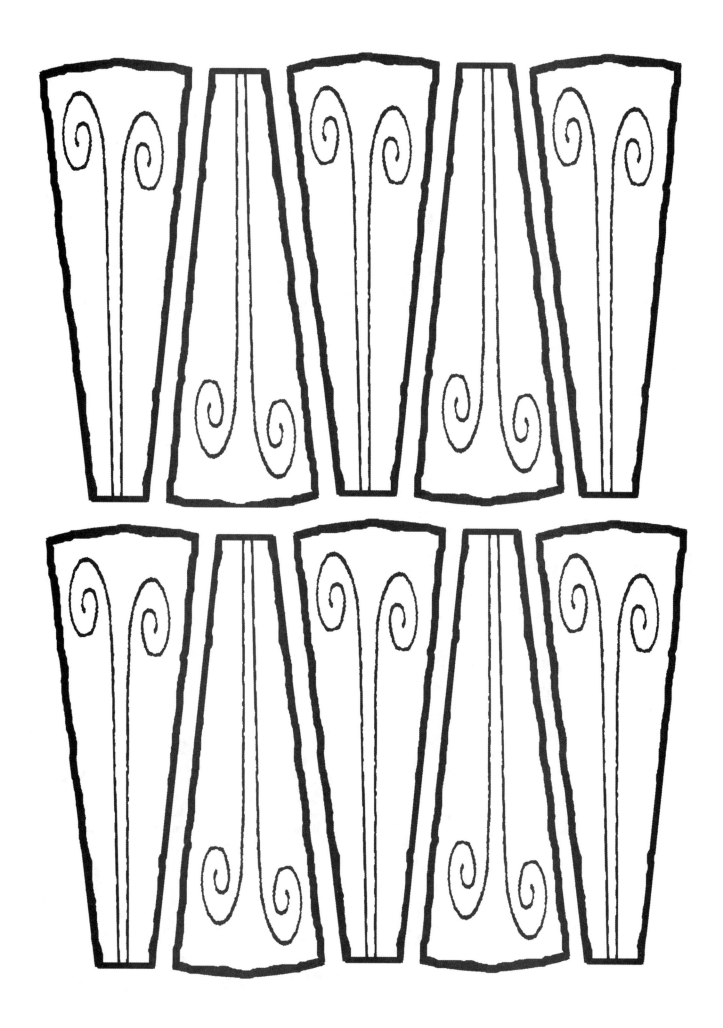

Cut carefully along the inside of the dotted line.

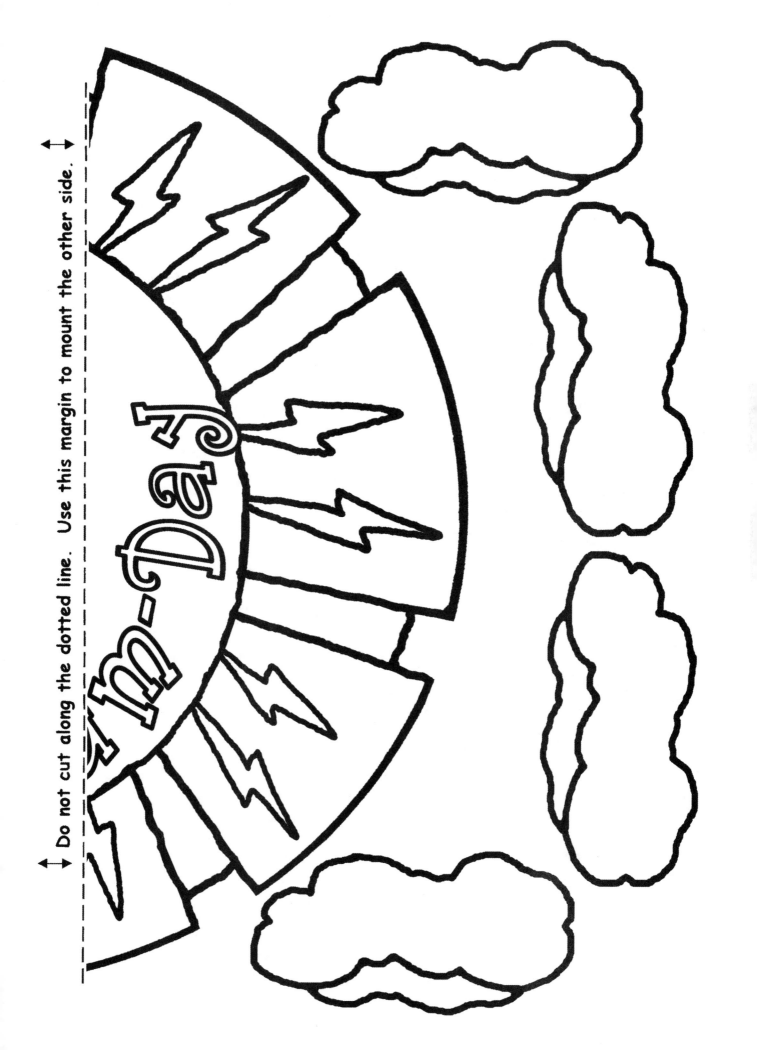

Do not cut along the dotted line. Use this margin to mount the other side.

Jim-Day

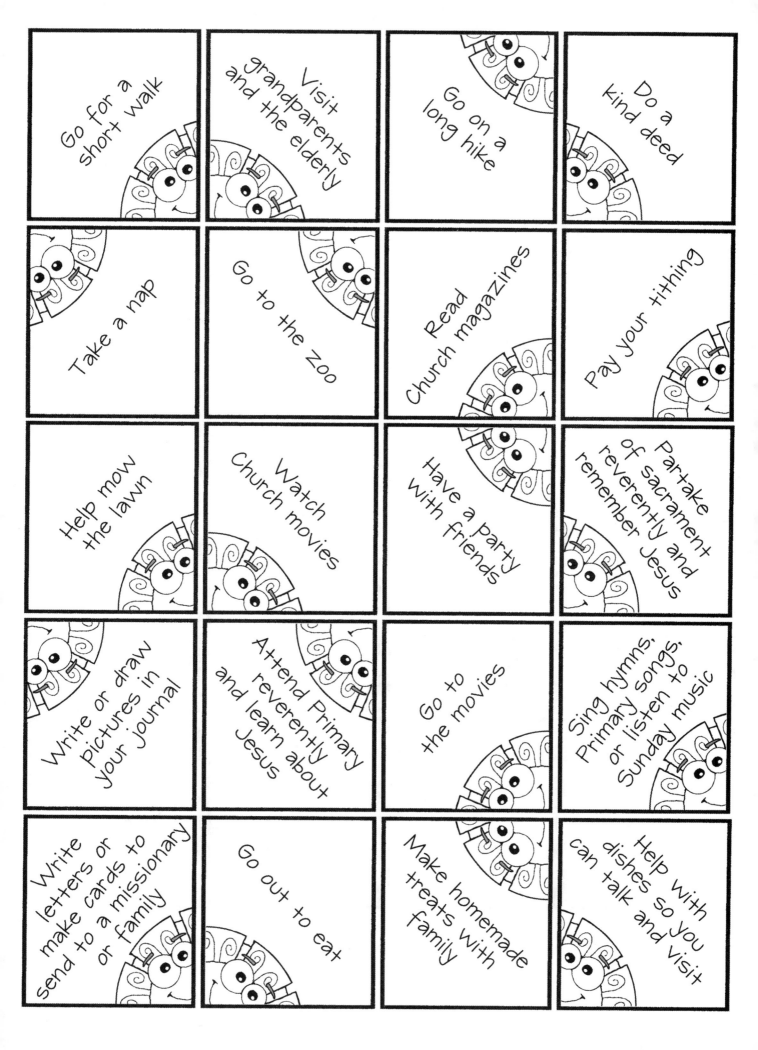

Go for a short walk

Visit grandparents and the elderly

Go on a long hike

Do a kind deed

Take a nap

Go to the zoo

Read Church magazines

Pay your tithing

Help mow the lawn

Watch Church movies

Have a party with friends

Partake of sacrament reverently and remember Jesus

Write or draw pictures in your journal

Attend Primary reverently and learn about Jesus

Go to the movies

Sing hymns, Primary songs, or listen to Sunday music

Write letters or make cards to send to a missionary or family

Go out to eat

Make homemade treats with family

Help with dishes so you can talk and visit

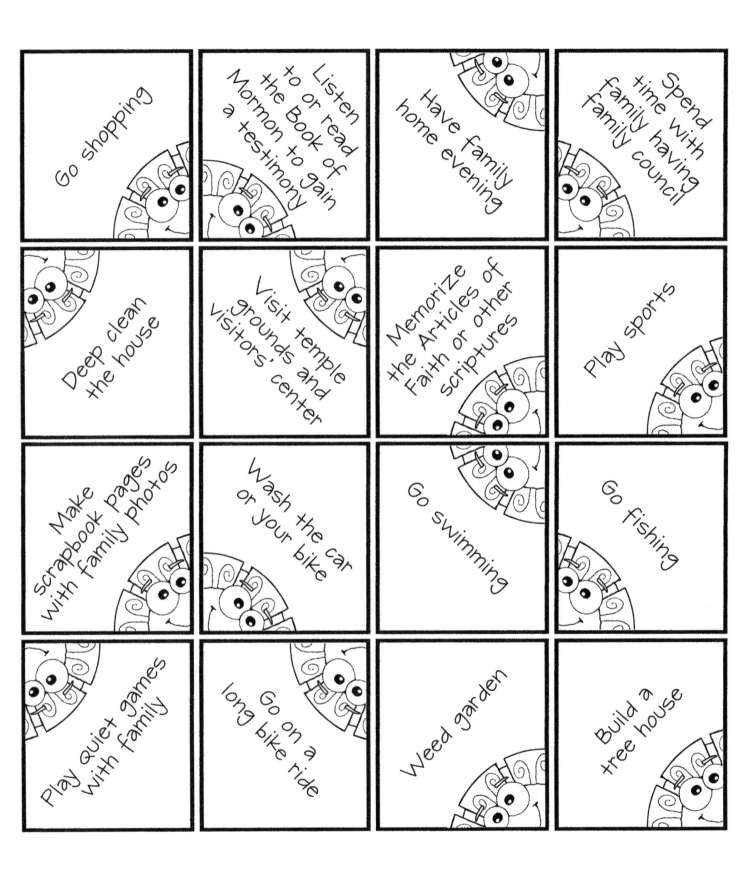

September—Theme 9: The Ten Commandments Teach Me to Love God and His Children

Practice Time:

Scripture Memorization—D&C 42:29

(shown left). Poster/cards (shown) are only available to <u>download from gospelgrabbag.com</u>.

Practice Song—Sing "Come Follow Me"

(*Hymns*, no. 116-shown right), **"Choose the Right Way"** (*Children's Songbook*, 160-161), **"Choose the Right"** (*Hymn*, no. 239), **"Stand for the Right"** (*Children's Songbook*, 159), and/or using the song visuals. These are only available to <u>download from gospelgrabbag.com</u>.

COME FOLLOW ME

SHARING TIME, Week 3:
I Should Honor My Parents

Activity: Are You Honor Off?
(Honor Parents Vote Casting)

OBJECTIVE: Help children learn the good ways to honor their parents and the bad things that show they are not honoring their parents. *Activity supports this message:* "Young people, if you honor your parents, you will love them, respect them, confide in them, be considerate of them, express appreciation for them, and demonstrate all of these things by following their counsel in righteousness and by obeying the commandments of God" (Dallin H. Oaks, "Honor Thy Father and Thy Mother," *Ensign*, May 1991).

TO MAKE VISUALS:

Copy, color, and cut out the Honor Parents sign and heart situation cards that follow. Mount sign on a poster and laminate the entire poster. Laminate hearts and attach double-stick tape to the backs of each. You'll need a bell or buzzer to ring.

ACTIVITY:

1. Ahead of time, post the heart situation cards around the room or under children's chairs or on the side of the board.

2. Talk to children about the objective above and how important a commandment to "honor thy father and thy mother" is. Talk about the promise that "thy days may be long upon the land" (Exodus 20:12).

3. Tell children that every day we make decisions to honor our parents or to not honor them. Each decision has a consequence. Blessings come from honoring them. Point to the sign and ask, "Are your actions on or off when it comes to honoring your parents?"

CAST YOUR VOTE:

1. Tell children, "Let's see if you really know how to honor your parents." Have children choose a heart from under their chair or posted in the room and read it aloud.

2. Then child votes by ringing a buzzer or bell <u>quickly</u> to show they are enthusiastically in favor of this action as a RIGHT way to HONOR YOUR PARENTS. Then post heart under the sign "Are You Honor Off? (On or Off). Honoring Parents Is Right On!"

3. If the action is a WRONG way to treat parents and is not honoring them, then children can quickly say, "E-RRRRRRR!" before the child says NO. Then the child posts the action under the poster (upside down).

Honor Otis Are You

Cut carefully along inside of dotted line.

Honoring
Parents Is
Right
On!

Do not cut along dotted line.   Use this margin to mount other side.

Andrew knew his grandfather well and remembered him telling him before he died to always choose the right. One day Andrew was tempted to do as his friend was doing, but he remembered his grandfather's wish and said no.

Ruth was supposed to go to her grandmother's house on the way home from school and told her mother she would. But her friends coaxed her into going to their house instead. Her grandmother was at home waiting for her to show up.

Mimi hit her brother on purpose when Mom wasn't looking. When he cried, Mimi told her mom it was just an accident.

Tristan's dad told him that if ever he had a problem he could come to him; no matter what time of day it was or if he was at work, he could call him. One day he had a decision to make and wasn't quite sure if he should say yes or no. So he decided to call his dad to check.

Hugs and kisses were Harrison's favorite things to get from his mom when he was little. But now that he was older, he would get embarrassed when his mom reached out for a kiss. It was time to get on the bus, and he had to run, but he turned around and blew a kiss to mom.

Bradley's friend had a problem and needed help. Bradley said, "Let's go ask my mom; she will know what to do."

Jacob knew his dad was really smart, especially when it came to choosing good friends and making good decisions. One day he wasn't sure about a certain friend's actions, and he later asked his dad what to do if it happened again.

Hailey listened to her mother in family home evening when she talked about being obedient. But Hailey wanted to see what it would feel like to break a commandment. She thought about what she would do, then knew it would make her mom sad, so she chose the right instead.

"Always be honest with others and yourself," said Landon's dad. But today was his math test, and he didn't study. So before the test, he placed the answers outside his backpack-just enough that he could see. "It won't hurt just once; I'll study harder next time," he thought.

Daniel's mother taught him to never tell a lie. But Daniel wanted to impress his friends and tell them he passed his math test. Before he could say so, he imagined his mother trusting him, so he said he didn't do well on the test.

Megan loved to dance at the recitals. This time she did everything just right, but her friend slipped. Instead of going on, she remembered her grandmother said to help others. But if she stopped to help, it would mean she wouldn't do as well, but she helped her friend anyway.

Alexa wanted to go to her soccer game on Saturday, but it was also her brother's soccer playoffs, and her mother told her she needed to be there. She felt sad she couldn't go to her game, but she honored her mother's wish to support her brother.

Austin's mother asked him to quickly get his homework done before he went to his friend's. Austin didn't want to do his homework and said, "Stop ordering me around and telling me what to do!"

Toby's mom trusted him to get his brother on the school bus each morning. Toby's brother was slow getting ready, and Toby ran ahead to meet his friends. So his brother missed the bus.

Kimberly said, "Bye, Mom, love you!" when she left for school. But when she was with her friends, she told them her mom was stupid for not buying her the short skirt she wanted.

Benjamin's father taught him in family home evening not to steal. One day he saw his brother and friends take gum from the store. So he pulled out some money and gave it to the guys to go back and pay.

Kelly could see that his mom could use some help emptying the garbage, but he let her do it anyway.

Isabella loved birthday presents and nagged her mother to get her a special bike, even though her mother was saving up for the new dress she needed. She said she just had to have the bike.

Lance told his dad that he would help his little sister clean her room, but his friends came early, so he decided to ignore his request.

Craig heard his friend Scott tell his mom that she looked pretty. When Craig got home, he noticed that his mother looked nice, but he decided she already knew it, so he said nothing.

Alexa liked to cut out princess paper dolls even though she knew Mom told her to clean her room. Company was coming, and she just wanted so much to cut out one more outfit, but she decided to clean her room instead.

Levi's mother scolded him for not picking up his things, but his friends were ringing the doorbell. "It's time for my big game, Mom, I don't have time," he said as he ran out the door.

Sam really liked to play certain games with his friends, and one day there was a game in which his friends liked to swear while they played. Sam remembered his dad said not to swear or use bad words, so he said, "I don't want to swear."

Sadie loved sitting by the window on the way home from school, and this day her brother said it was his turn. She knew it was, but she yelled back, "It's my turn, Mom."

September—Theme 9:
The Ten Commandments Teach Me to Love God and His Children

Practice Time Activities to download from gospelgrabbag.com (shown on p. 90):

. *Scripture Memorization*—D&C **42:29** Posters/cards

. *Practice Song*—Sing "**Come Follow Me**" (*Hymns*, no. 116), "**Choose the Right Way**"
(*Children's Songbook, 160-161*), "**Choose the Right**" (*Hymns*, no. 239), and "**Stand for the Right**" (*CS*, 159), using song visuals

---

SHARING TIME, Week 4: *I Should Respect Others*
Activity: Respect/Disrespect (Choices Match Game)

OBJECTIVE: Help children know the difference between respect and disrespect and ways we can show respect and kindness toward others.

TO MAKE VISUALS:
Copy, color, and cut out the signs and choice cards that follow.

ACTIVITY:

1. Have children choose a card and place it under the I CAN SHOW RESPECT or the I SHOULD NOT SHOW DISRESPECT sign.

2. Leader then asks when each card is posted, "How does this show respect?" "How does this show disrespect?" "What are the consequences for making this decision?"

Examples of consequences for decisions:

"I CAN SHOW RESPECT"

. SHOW REVERENCE—By folding our arms during prayer, we are showing our Heavenly Father that we want to listen to what is being said and want to have God's blessings.

. PRAY APPROPRIATELY—The Holy Ghost can teach us things we need to know.

. DRESS MODESTLY—It shows that we know our body is a temple and is very sacred. When we are clean and wear our Sunday-best clothes to church, we are showing respect for Heavenly Father when we enter His house.

. BE KIND TO OTHERS—Others will be kind to you, and you can feel at peace.

. USE GOOD WORDS—It's hard if you use bad words because you can't take them back.

. LISTEN POLITELY—We can learn things we need to do to be happy.

. SAY THANK YOU—Others will feel appreciated and loved.

"I SHOULD NOT SHOW DISRESPECT"

. FORGET TO SAY PLEASE—Others may not be so willing to help you.

. IGNORE PARENTS—They may not trust you to do as they ask.

. INTERRUPT OTHERS—They cannot finish what they are doing, wasting their time.

. DEMAND TO EAT—Others may not be so willing to prepare meals for you.

. CALL OTHERS BAD NAMES—This hurts others, and they will not want to be your friend.

I can

RESI

I should

DISRE

Cut carefully along inside of dotted line.

show

PECT

not show

SPECT

Show Reverence

Pray Appropriately

Be Kind to Others

Use Good Words

Say Thank You

Forget to Say Please

Interrupt Others

Demand to Eat

Dress Modestly

Listen Politely

Ignore Parents

Call Others Bad Names

I'm Kayla. My great aunt Sadie was two months old when her mother died, so a minister and his wife adopted her. I want her to be baptized a member of the Church. Can you help me find her?

I'm Aunt Sadie. I learned that the gospel is true in the spirit world. I am anxiously waiting for my baptism day. Can you find my great niece Kayla so she can do my baptism?

I'm Takashi. My grandma and grandpa Nishijima lived in Japan. They were good people but died without hearing the gospel. I want to enter their names in the temple so they can be sealed together. Can you help me find them?

We are Fern and Colleen. Our parents have had their temple work done, but we have not been sealed to them. We want to be a forever family, but we need Emily's help. Can you help us find her?

I'm Emily. While reading my family history, I learned that my grandmother's Uncle Clayton had two daughters, Fern and Colleen, who died of scarlet fever when they were nine and eleven years old. They need to be baptized and sealed to their parents. Can you help me find them?

We're Grandma and Grandpa Nishijima. Our grandson Takashi is trying to send our names to the temple. We want to be sealed quickly so we can be together forever. Can you help us find him?

I'm Jenny. My friend Amanda was killed in a car crash when she was nine years old. She was not a member of the Church, and I want to be baptized for her in the temple. So can you help me find her?

I'm Amanda. My friend Jenny told me about Jesus Christ. I wanted to be baptized but didn't have a chance as I was killed in a car crash. Since I only have a spirit body now, I can't be baptized, so would you find Jenny for me so she can be baptized for me?

I'm Ronnie. My uncle Leroy was a rebellious boy when he drowned in a river near our home. If he had lived longer, he might have accepted the gospel and been baptized. I hope he would like me to be baptized for him, so will you help me find him?

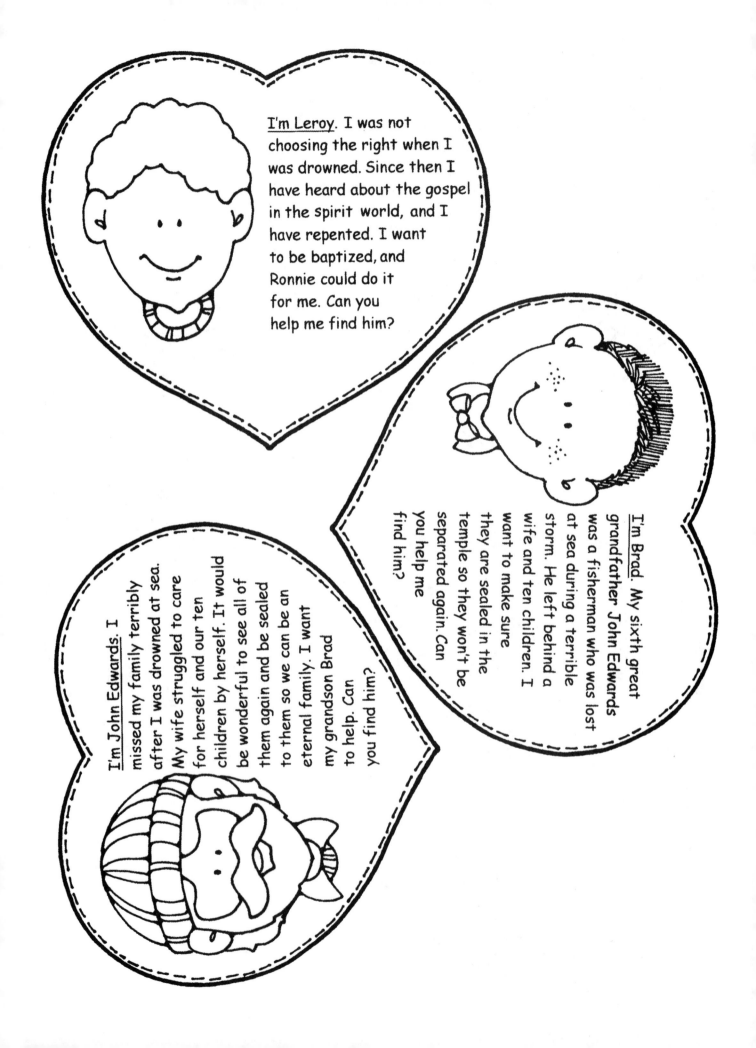

I'm Leroy. I was not choosing the right when I was drowned. Since then I have heard about the gospel in the spirit world, and I have repented. I want to be baptized, and Ronnie could do it for me. Can you help me find him?

I'm Brad. My sixth great grandfather John Edwards was a fisherman who was lost at sea during a terrible storm. He left behind a wife and ten children. I want to make sure they are sealed in the temple so they won't be separated again. Can you help me find him?

I'm John Edwards. I missed my family terribly after I was drowned at sea. My wife struggled to care for herself and our ten children by herself. It would be wonderful to see all of them again and be sealed to them so we can be an eternal family. I want my grandson Brad to help. Can you find him?

I'm Harrison. My second great-grandfather Marshall Jeffers fought in the Civil War. He gave his life so other men might know freedom. I need to find more information so I can complete his record and send it to the temple. Can you help me find him?

I'm Marshall. I was killed in the large battle at Gettysburg. In the spirit world, I have been learning about Jesus Christ, and I want to follow Him. I need to have my temple work done, and my grandson Harrison will do it. Can you help me find him?

I'm Judy. I was checking my family history and noticed that the temple work was done for the Colton Harris family, except for their little boy, James. He was missed because he was born after the family immigrated to America. I want to make sure he is with his family. So can you help me find him?

I'm James. I have been waiting to join my family for a very long time. All of their work has been done, but my name was not on the record in England, so I was not included in the family sealing. I have a relative named Judy who does her family history and hope she will find the mistake. Can you help me find her?

I'm Stella. My great-grandmother Ethel Petersen wrote in her journal about the roses she planted outside her home in Denmark. She was 93 when she heard the gospel. She wanted to be baptized but died before she had the chance. I want to make sure she is baptized. Can you help me find her?

I'm Ethel Petersen. My great granddaughter Stella cared enough to read my journal and find out I died before I was baptized. I enjoyed my lovely rose garden, but I didn't have the chance to enjoy the beauty of the gospel. Will you help me find her so she can be baptized for me?

November—Theme 11:
I Can Choose to Be a Missionary Now

Practice Time:

Scripture Memorization—Mark 16:15
(shown left). Poster/cards (shown) are only available to download from gospelgrabbag.com.

Practice Song—Sing "I Hope They Call Me on a Mission" (*Children's Songbook*, 169-shown right) and **"We'll Bring the World His Truth"** (*Children's Songbook*, 172) song visuals. These are only available to download from gospelgrabbag.com.

SHARING TIME, Week 1: **I Can Be a Missionary by Serving Others**
Activity: I will be a Serv"ant" (Toss and Tell)

TO PRESENT – Parts 1 and 2:

Part #1 STORY / VIDEO: You may want to consider showing this video. To find video, go to Google.com and type in "The Coat: A Story of Charity") a true story of President Heber J. Grant. "President Heber J. Grant's father died when President Grant was just nine days old. His mother was very poor and earned money by sewing for other people. Sometimes she sewed for so many hours without resting that she could hardly push the pedal of her sewing machine. Heber would often crawl under the sewing machine to push the pedal for her. The winters were very cold, and Heber had only a thin, worn coat to keep him warm. He longed to have a warm coat but knew they barely had enough money for food. He was delighted on his birthday when his mother gave him a warm coat she had sewn. It was his most prized possession. A few weeks later, Heber saw a boy shivering with cold, and he remembered how it felt. He took off his new coat and gave it to the boy" (see video on youtube). Matthew 25:40 is the scripture featured in the video.

Part #2 TOSS AND TELL ACTIVITY: To do the activity, place the Serv"ant" Sack 2-3 feet away from the children (behind a line—taped on the floor). Give each child three raisins, telling them the raisins look like ants. Have them toss the raisins into the sack to see if they can be good Serv"ant"s. Before tossing the three ants, have them tell one way they can serve others, including their families (serving God). Give each child a point for each raisin/ant tossed into sack. Divide into teams to play, awarding points at the end.

I Will Be a Serv"ant"!

Do not cut along dotted line. Use this margin to mount other side.

Gospelgrabbag.com

Gospelgrabbag.com

November—Theme 11:
I Can Choose to Be a Missionary Now

Practice Time Activities to download from gospelgrabbag.com (shown on p. 59):

. *Scripture Memorization*—Mark 16:15 Posters/cards

. *Practice Song*—Sing "I Hope They Call Me on a Mission" (Children's Songbook, 169)
using song visuals

SHARING TIME, Week 3: *I Can Teach My Friends about Jesus and His Church*
Activity: Share the Gospel (Testimony Spin-the-Bottle)

OBJECTIVE: Encourage children to bear their testimony about Heavenly Father, Jesus Christ, Joseph Smith, the Sabbath day, the living prophet, temples, the Book of Mormon, and the priesthood.

TO MAKE VISUALS:

Copy, color, and cut out the testimony spin-the-bottle chart. Follow instructions to cut out and put chart together. Mount the chart on a poster and laminate the entire poster. Laminate the bottle/arrow. Place a paper fastener in the center of the bottle and through chart, making sure the fastener is loose so the bottle will spin.

ACTIVITY:

1. Tell children, "Heavenly Father sent us to this earth with a testimony of His plan and of the gospel of Jesus Christ, but when we came, a veil was placed over our minds so we could live by faith. When we hear truth, the Holy Ghost will let us know. We will feel a warm feeling in our heart, and our mind will know that it is true. When we read the scriptures or hear others bear their testimony, we can know if they are true, especially if we pray for the Spirit to be with us."

2. Ask children, "Have any of your friends asked you about your church, about what you believe in?" Point to the chart and say: **"Don't Bottle Up Your Testimony . . . Share It!** Let's play Testimony Spin-the-Bottle so we can share our testimonies."

3. Have children take turns coming up and spinning the bottle to point to a testimony subject (e.g., BOOK OF MORMON), then share their testimony on the subject. If one subject has been covered several times, turn it to the next subject that has not been expressed.

Testimony Variation: There are many ways children can bear their testimony for this activity:
• Tell what they know to be true • Sing a verse of a song • Recite an Article of Faith or scripture (have some ready to read) • Tell a story or share an experience • Tell about another person's testimony or a testimony of someone in the scriptures (e.g., Alma, Abinadi, or Ammon)

Don't Bottle Up

Living Prophet

Jesus Christ

Sabbath Day

Heavenly Father

SUNDAY

Shar

Your Testimony...

Joseph Smith

Temples

Cut carefully along the inside of the dotted line.

Do not cut along the dotted line. Use this margin to mount the other side.

December—Theme 12: Jesus Christ Is the Son of God

Behold, I am Jesus Christ, the Son of God. I am the life and the light of the world.

D&C 11:28

Practice Time:
Scripture Memorization—D&C **11:28** (shown left). Poster/cards (shown) are only available to <u>download from gospelgrabbag.com</u>.

Practice Song—Sing "**He Sent His Son**" (*Children's Songbook,* 34-35) using the song visuals (shown right). These are only available to <u>download from gospelgrabbag.com</u>.

HE SENT HIS SON

SHARING TIME, Week 2:
Jesus Grew in Wisdom and Stature and in Favor with God and Man

Activity: I Can Grow to Be Like Jesus
(Inch-by-Inch Growth Chart)

OBJECTIVE: Help children grow to become like Jesus: grow in wisdom, stature, and in favor with God and man (Luke 2:53; D&C 88:118; 89:20; 88:63; Proverbs 18:24). With this activity, children can reflect words in a mirror that show how Jesus lived and reflect upon their own countenance to remind themselves to be like Jesus.

TO MAKE VISUALS:
Copy, color, and cut out the Jesus growth chart pieces and ruler wordstrip (with words spelled backward), plus a bookmark that follows for each child. Laminate visuals. You'll need a hand-held mirror or table mirror children can look into to look at the ruler and see backward words. To make bookmarks for children, fold them in half and glue back to back to back. Do not laminate.

ACTIVITY:
1. Ask children, "When you have a choice, do you ask yourself, 'What would Jesus do?'" This is the question we can ask each day so we can try to be like Jesus. From the time Jesus was a baby and then a small boy, Jesus grew in wisdom and stature and favor with God and man.

2. As you talk about the four areas in which Jesus increased, have children help you place the puzzle (growth chart) puzzle pieces on the board. Talk about climbing inch-by-inch each day in all the areas Jesus grew. Talk about how when Jesus was a boy, He had to learn things His parents and Church leaders taught Him—just like we do. As He grew older, He prayed and asked Heavenly Father how He should grow and what He should do. We too can be like Jesus to increase in these areas. Have a child read Luke 2:52.

3. Have children take turns drawing a ruler wordstrip. Children can then take a mirror and look into it to see their reflection as they say, "I can grow to be like Jesus as I . . . (then read the words by reflecting them in the mirror to read them forward).

4. Then have child place the ruler where it goes on the chart to match the "And Jesus increased in wisdom . . . and stature . . . and in favor with God . . . and man puzzle pieces (as shown). To make it easy for the leader, he/she can look at the code W (wisdom) S (stature), G (God), or M (man) to know if this is correct. For example, the "I obey my parents" letter M wordstrip will be placed next to the . . . and man puzzle piece.

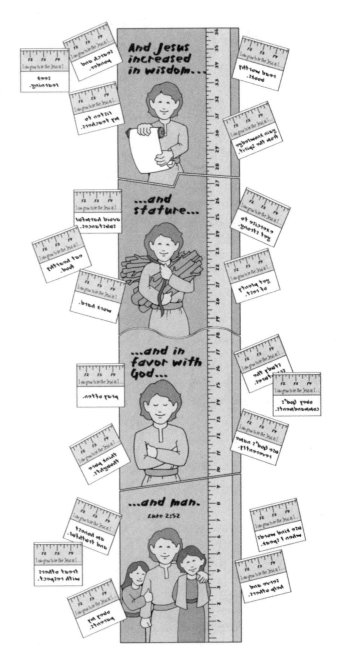

Bookmark: Give children bookmark (shown below) to write ways they can measure up and grow to be like Jesus.

Card 1 (top left)

12   13   14

I can grow to be like Jesus as I . . .

search and ponder.

Card 2 (top right)

12   13   14

I can grow to be like Jesus as I . . .

seek learning.

Card 3 (middle left)

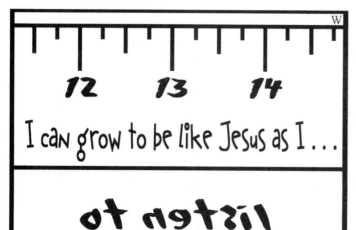

12   13   14

I can grow to be like Jesus as I . . .

listen to my teachers.

Card 4 (middle right)

12   13   14

I can grow to be like Jesus as I . . .

read worthy books.

Card 5 (bottom)

12   13   14

I can grow to be like Jesus as I . . .

gain knowledge from the Spirit.

Card 1 (top left):

12 13 14

I can grow to be like Jesus as I . . .

avoid harmful substances.

Card 2 (top right):

12 13 14

I can grow to be like Jesus as I . . .

eat healthy food.

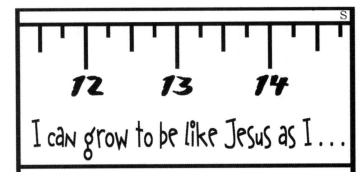

Card 3 (middle left):

12 13 14

I can grow to be like Jesus as I . . .

exercise to get strong.

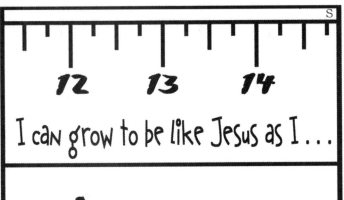

Card 4 (middle right):

12 13 14

I can grow to be like Jesus as I . . .

get plenty of rest.

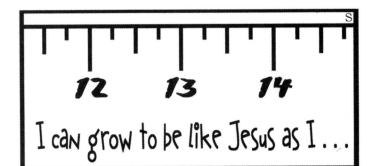

Card 5 (bottom):

12 13 14

I can grow to be like Jesus as I . . .

work hard.

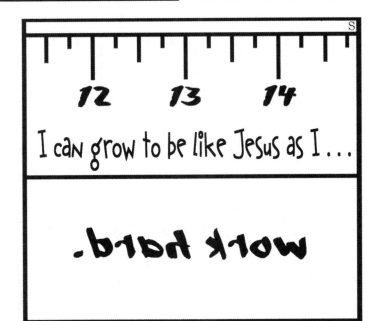

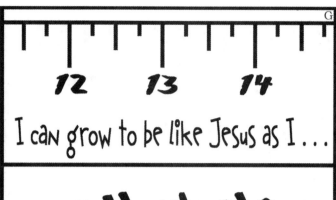

12 13 14

I can grow to be like Jesus as I . . .

study the scriptures.

12 13 14

I can grow to be like Jesus as I . . .

pray often.

12 13 14

I can grow to be like Jesus as I . . .

obey God's commandments.

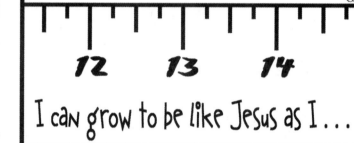

12 13 14

I can grow to be like Jesus as I . . .

think pure thoughts.

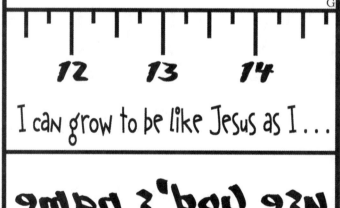

12 13 14

I can grow to be like Jesus as I . . .

use God's name reverently.

Card 1

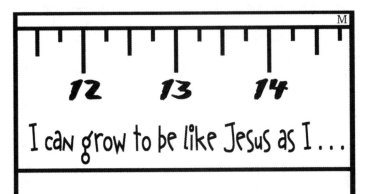

12   13   14

I can grow to be like Jesus as I . . .

am honest
and truthful.

Card 2

12   13   14

I can grow to be like Jesus as I . . .

treat others
with respect.

Card 3

12   13   14

I can grow to be like Jesus as I . . .

obey my
parents.

Card 4

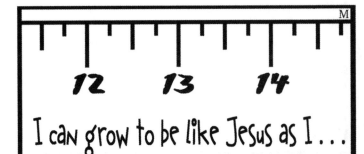

12   13   14

I can grow to be like Jesus as I . . .

use kind words
when I speak.

Card 5

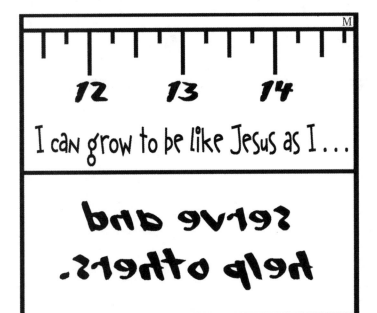

12   13   14

I can grow to be like Jesus as I . . .

serve and
help others.

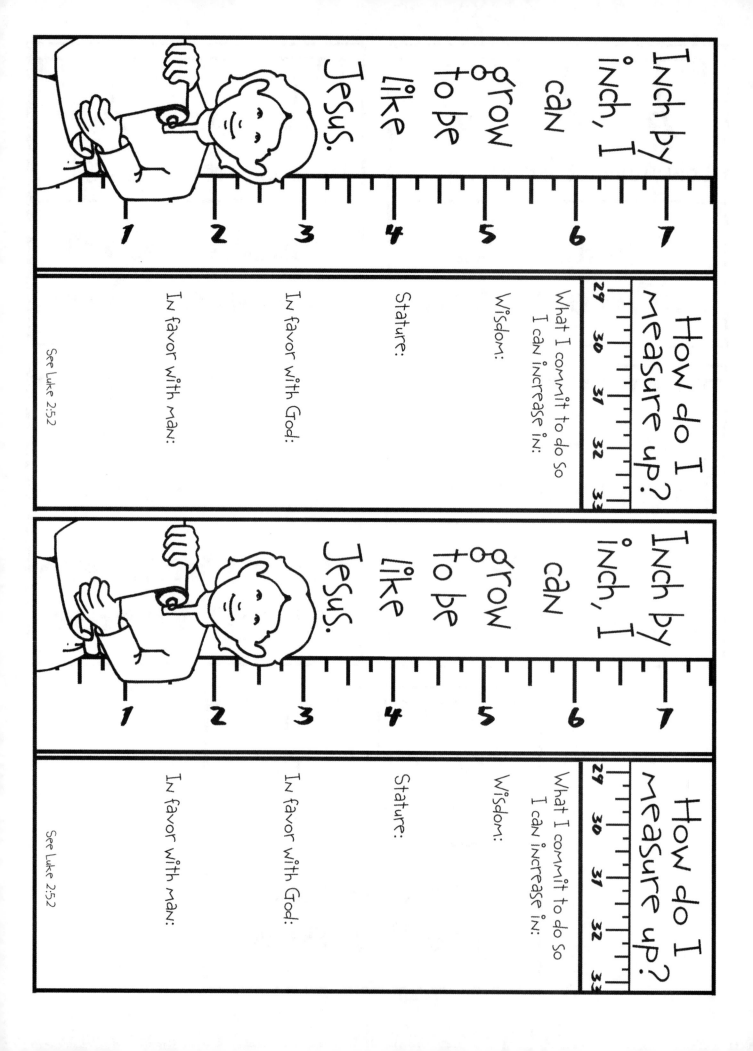

Inch by inch, I can grow to be like Jesus.

1 2 3 4 5 6 7

See Luke 2:52

How do I measure up?

29 30 31 32 33

What I commit to do so I can increase in:

Wisdom:

Stature:

In favor with God:

In favor with man:

Inch by inch, I can grow to be like Jesus.

1 2 3 4 5 6 7

See Luke 2:52

How do I measure up?

29 30 31 32 33

What I commit to do so I can increase in:

Wisdom:

Stature:

In favor with God:

In favor with man:

December—Theme 12:
Jesus Christ Is the Son of God

Practice Time Activities to download from gospelgrabbag.com (shown on p. 129):
. *Scripture Memorization*—D&C 11:28 Posters/cards
. *Practice Song*—Sing "He Sent His Son" (*Children's Songbook,* 34-35) using song visuals

---

SHARING TIME, Week 4: **Joseph Smith Saw and Testified of Jesus Christ**
Activity: Because Joseph Smith Restored the Gospel
(*Testimony Quiz*)

OBJECTIVE: Help children bear testimony of the restored gospel of Jesus Christ. They can prepare to bear testimony by pondering the statements that follow. Each statement begins, "Because of the Restoration . . .," then names a certain part of the gospel that blesses us today.

TO MAKE VISUALS:
Copy, color, and cut out the Because of the Restoration quiz match cards that follow, cutting down the middle wavy line. Laminate.

ACTIVITY:
1. Tell children, "When Jesus Christ was on the earth, He chose twelve Apostles and reestablished His Church. Jesus died and was resurrected, eventually returning to heaven. After the Apostles died, there was a great Apostasy when many of the people stopped believing in Jesus. Because of the Apostasy, Heavenly Father withdrew priesthood authority and other important parts of the Church from the earth. This time was called the "Dark Ages."

Activity: Because Joseph Smith Restored the Gospel
(Testimony Quiz)

2. Tell children, "When Joseph Smith followed God and restored the Church of Jesus Christ, the priesthood and other important parts of the gospel were brought back (D&C 20:8-12). Jesus said the restored gospel would be like a light in the darkness (read D&C 45:28)."

3. Get ready to show matched cards. Tell children, "Because of the restoration of the gospel, we can enjoy special blessings today. Let's find out which things were restored and the blessings they bring." Summarize them as follows, "We have (holding up matched cards): the Book of Mormon, baptism, a living prophet, the Melchizedek Priesthood, the plan of salvation, an understanding of the Godhead, forever families, missionaries, the gift of the Holy Ghost, the Word of Wisdom, tithing, and family home evening."

4. Read a complete sample card (e.g., show part one: "Because of the Restoration . . . the Book of Mormon was translated by Joseph Smith through the power of God." Then show part two: ". . . We now have a sacred record that contains the fulness of the gospel and is another testament of Jesus Christ.").

Quiz: (1) Divide children into two teams. (2) Mix up the cards, and tape them facedown on the board. (3) Have teams take turns having a player come up and turn two cards over to make a match. Once a match is made, read the cards aloud and post them on the board faceup.

Because of the Restoration...

the Book of Mormon was translated by Joseph Smith, through the power of God.

The Book of Mormon
Another Testament of Jesus Christ

Because of the Restoration...

... We now have a sacred record that contains the fulness of the gospel and another testament of Jesus Christ.

Because of the Restoration...

the Aaronic Priesthood was restored by John the Baptist to Joseph Smith and Oliver Cowdery.

Because of the Restoration...

... The power and authority to baptize is once again on the earth.

Because of the Restoration...

we have a living prophet on the earth today.

... He receives revelation and guidance to help us navigate through difficult times.

Because of the Restoration...

the Melchizedek Priesthood was restored by Peter, James, and John to the Prophet Joseph Smith and Oliver Cowdery.

... Through this priesthood, worthy males can perform ordinances, ordain others, heal the sick, and pronounce blessings in the name of Jesus Christ.

Because of the Restoration...

we know about Heavenly Father's plan of salvation through scripture and revelation.

... We know that each of us is a child of God and that Jesus Christ is our Savior, and that we can live with Them forever if we do what is right.

Earth Life

Because of the Restoration...

the sealing power was restored by Moses, Elias, and Elijah to the Prophet Joseph Smith and Oliver Cowdery.

... Families that now live on the earth and family members that have died can be sealed together forever.

Because of the Restoration...

Joseph Smith received a revelation to call worthy men to preach the gospel.

... Missionaries—young men and women, senior sisters, and couples—take the gospel message throughout the world.

Because of the Restoration...

we have priesthood power to bestow the gift of the Holy Ghost after baptism.

... With the Holy Ghost, we have the power of discernment to know right from wrong and to receive direction and comfort when needed.

Because of the Restoration...

Joseph Smith received a vision and saw Heavenly Father and His Son, Jesus Christ.

... We have learned that Heavenly Father and Jesus Christ each has a body of flesh and bone and that each is an individual and distinct Being.

Gospelgrabbag.com

Because of the Restoration...

Joseph Smith prayed and received a revelation called the Word of Wisdom.

... We have a commandment for diet and health that will bless our physical bodies and help us receive spiritual blessings.

Because of the Restoration...

the prophet Lorenzo Snow encouraged us to pay tithing to build up the kingdom of God on the earth.

... We can build temples and churches to do the Lord's work, and in return, Heavenly Father has promised to open the windows of heaven to shower down blessings on us.

Because of the Restoration...

the prophet Joseph F. Smith counseled Church members to hold family home evening.

... We can pray and learn the gospel together as a family, growing in unity and love.

Charity